Wrestle and Win is a must read to achieve a level of high school succ compete and succeed at the collegiat read for coaches, parents and fans so they can assist in creating and implementing a plan to help the young wrestlers achieve their potential and meet their goals. Steve Kimpel's personal experiences as a competitor, college coach and recruiter and administrator, combined with his academic accomplishments, certainly qualify him as a respected expert in the sport whose advice is certainly worth following. I highly recommend this book.

R. Wayne Baughman
Three-time Olympic competitor and two-time coach of the U.S. Olympic team
NCAA Champion and NCAA Div I Coach (27 years)

My goal as a coach is to train my wrestlers as efficiently and effectively as possible. This book hits the nail right on the head for how you can be efficient and effective in your wrestling training.

Mike Clayton
2009 Centennial Conference Coach of the Year
2008 NCAA Rookie Coach of the Year
Author of The Championship Training Log for Wrestling

Wrestle and Win is an outstanding roadmap to success for wrestlers of all levels. Follow the advice in this book and you will be a champion!

Ken Chertow
U.S.A. Olympian
Gold Medal Training Camp System

I found the book to be a great resource for any wrestler/coach. With your insight on training and match preparations this book will be a plus for any wrestler/coach. I found a great deal of information that I plan on using in my program here at Brandon HS. Any wrestler/coach looking to get to the next level will find this book very useful.

Russ Cozart
Head Wrestling Coach Brandon HS
83 State Champions, 20 Team State Titles
Dual Meet Record 437-1
7 time Fila-Veteran World Champion

Very informative for any coach or athlete trying to advance to the next level! I look forward to implementing some of the techniques in my own coaching.

Troy Steiner
NCAA Champion
Assistant Coach Oregon State University

Wrestle and Win

The Wrestler's Guide to Strength, Conditioning, Nutrition and College Preparation

Wrestle and Win

The Wrestler's Guide to Strength, Conditioning, Nutrition and College Preparation

BY
Steve Kimpel

Turtle Press   **Washington, DC**

To contact the author or to order additional copies of this book:
> Turtle Press
> 500 N. Washington St, #1545
> Rockville MD 20849.
> www.TurtlePress.com

Photos by Mark Bauer, Joseph Gosar, and Derek Montgomery.

ISBN 978-1-934903-20-9
LCCN 2010019920

Printed in the United States of America

Warning-Disclaimer

This book is designed to provide information on the strength, fitness and conditioning for wrestling. It is not the
purpose of this book to reprint all the information that is otherwise available to the author, publisher, printer or
distributors, but instead to compliment, amplify and supplement other texts. You are urged to read all available
material, learn as much as you wish about the subjects covered in this book and tailor the information to your
individual needs. Anyone practicing the skills, exercises, drills or techniques presented in this book should be
physically healthy enough to do so and have permission from a licensed physician before participating. Every
effort has been made to make this book as complete and accurate as possible. However, there may be mistakes,
both typographical and in content. Therefore, this text should be used only as a general guide and not as the
ultimate source of information on the subjects presented here in this book on any topic, skill or subject. The
purpose of this book is to provide information and entertain. The author, publisher, printer and distributor shall
neither have liability nor responsibility to any person or entity with respect to loss or damages caused, or alleged
to have been caused, directly or indirectly, by the information contained in this book. If you do not wish to be
bound by the above, you may return this book to the publisher for a full refund.

Cataloging in Publication data

Kimpel, Steve.
 Wrestle and win : the wrestler's guide to strength, conditioning, nutrition and college
preparation / by Steve Kimpel.
     p. cm.
 ISBN 978-1-934903-20-9
1. Wrestling--United States. 2. Wrestling--Nutritional aspects. 3. Universities and colleg-
es--Admission. 4. College sports--United States--History. I. Title.
 GV1195.K46 2010
 796.8120973--dc22

                              2010019920

Contents

To Julie, Courtney, Katrina, Kayla and Cody.
Thank you for your love and encouragement.

FOREWORD

Wrestling is a tough sport! When you compete, you are out there alone and you cannot rely on teammates to take up the slack if you get tired or to help you out if you're not fully prepared. Success requires a sustained commitment to working hard on and off the mat. Fortunately you can be in total control of the things that will make you a champion.

When I was an athlete, I discovered that I needed to focus on developing my strength and conditioning in ways that might have been different than some of my teammates. Even though I have had some of the best coaches in the world, I developed the most when I took responsibility for my own training. This means that I couldn't just go through a practice and be done. Most of the time there were things I needed extra work on.

In my years as a competitor and a coach, I've learned first-hand about the importance of a good strength training program and proper nutrition. If you do the right kind of training and work hard, you will condition your body and your mind. Every workout brings you closer to achieving your goals. You must have the discipline and the commitment to do what is necessary. Commitment is what separates the champions from their competitors.

I was fortunate to have had successes at many different levels of competition including the Olympic Games and world championships. Now I have the opportunity to coach. It is interesting that two wrestlers can be in the same training session and doing the same workouts, but they don't develop the same. The difference lies in how badly a wrestler wants to succeed and how hard he or she is willing to work to get there.

Wrestling has been an amazing journey for me. It has taught me things that I use every day. Following the advice in this book will make you more fit to wrestle and increase your chances of qualifying academically to get into the college of your choice. When you apply the lessons you learn from your training to the other areas of your life, you will be successful in almost any endeavor. You have heard the saying, "Once you've wrestled, everything else is easier." Life may be hard, but you will be tough enough to take it.

Dennis Hall, World Champion

PREFACE

In the 25 years since I began my career as a high school wrestler, I've watched hundreds of wrestlers and identified what makes them successful. The best wrestlers are different because of their commitment to getting the most out of themselves. After reading this book, you will learn what you can do on your own to increase your chances for success. Concepts in this book are proven training principles that will not only enhance your performance, but allow you to have a long, fulfilling career.

If you are reading this book you understand that distancing yourself from your competition requires that you do work outside of the normal practice time. After all, as a teammate of mine once pointed out, "Everyone practices at 3 p.m." Long-term success in wrestling requires a commitment to off-season conditioning activities, developing wrestling-specific strength and eating right. You probably work hard, but you may not be realizing your potential if your training methods are not specific to wrestling and appropriate for the time of the year you are in.

Your off-the-mat preparation falls into one of the three areas described in this book: Part I will teach you about conditioning and strength, Part II focuses on nutrition and weight management, and in Part III you will learn how to prepare academically for college and then how to get a college coach's attention.

Here are just a few things you will learn after reading this book:

- Training principles to help you create your own strength and conditioning workouts

- The best exercises for developing wrestling-specific strength

- How to make weight efficiently

- Questions to consider when evaluating supplements

- How to determine if college wrestling is for you

- What happens during the college recruiting process

This book will not only help you win matches, but following the advice will help you stay healthy and have a longer career. However, what you read may challenge things you currently believe about training for wrestling.

For example, many wrestlers do a lot of running or wrestle for long periods of time to get into shape. See chapter two to see why it is more important to train hard than to train long.

Have you noticed that when wrestling season starts many wrestling teams stop their heavy weight lifting and begin circuit training? Turn to chapter six to see a better way to develop strength during the season.

Do you drink a sports drink like Gatorade during wrestling practice? Check out chapter seven to see why you should and to get a recipe for making your own.

Most athletes' strength programs have traditional weight room exercises, but after reading chapter five you will have a whole new philosophy about developing wrestling-specific strength.

After you take the quiz in chapter 10, you should have a pretty good idea if college wrestling is for you and how you can begin preparing immediately to be recruited. During my years as a college coach, I saw many wrestlers who were good enough to wrestle in college, but who were not at all prepared to be recruited. In most cases these wrestlers were smart enough to succeed in college, but had not taken the right classes in high school or earned the grades they needed. In other cases, they didn't know how to get the attention of college coaches who tend to only focus on the multi-time state champions.

After you read this book, you will know how to go about contacting a coach and the important things that you should do during your visits to colleges. I have even included sample letters to college coaches to give you an idea of how to write your own.

Although I have included workouts, meal plans, and examples of letters to college coaches for you to immediately use, I hope you will adapt these to meet your specific needs. You will learn many new things as you read, but your understanding and your success will increase as you develop your own strategies for achieving your goals.

Best of luck in your training, I will be watching for you on the championship side of the bracket!

Steve Kimpel, Ph.D.
Rexburg, Idaho

ACKNOWLEDGEMENTS

I'd like to thank the following people for their assistance on this project. Julie Kimpel and Lynn Kimpel have invested their time, usually with little forewarning from me, to review drafts and provide feedback. Keven Glider, Kimball Mason, and Josh Sirucek provided excellent feedback on the manuscript. A special thanks to my high school wrestling coach and English teacher, Scott Zurfluh, who also reviewed the manuscript. His candid feedback about my wrestling, my work in his classes, and the choices I made in my life continue to be a guiding influence on me. Joseph Gosar dedicated countless hours shooting and editing most of the pictures of the exercises. Derek Montgomery and Marc Bauer were kind enough to provide me with action shots of wrestlers they had photographed. Jacob Larsen and Jeff Von Haden secured permission for use of many of the athletes pictured in the book. Lucas and Cammie Ingram believed in the project and provided me access to a location for photography. The following individuals served as models for the exercise pictures: Sterling Glines, Paxton Ingram, Ben and Mark Orchard, Jessie Smith, Tom Stickley, Cameron Weekes, and Kristopher Wilson.

PART ONE

Conditioning and Strength

CHAPTER 1
Training Smart

Have you ever wondered how to organize everything you know about exercise to make it into an effective training program? Wrestling requires agility, balance, coordination, power, reaction time, speed, and strength. Not all of these performance attributes are needed in equal amounts, however. The amount of each depends on several factors. As you read, you will learn how to train yourself to enhance your strengths and improve your weaknesses.

This chapter will highlight three training essentials which are fundamental to all the adaptations your body makes as you get into shape. Understanding the first training essential, "Basic Principles," is important in the overall design of your workouts. The second essential, "Muscle Fibers and Performance," describes basic differences between the muscles in a person's body and how various kinds of training specifically maximize their potential. Finally, "Energy Systems" explains the different ways that your body makes energy depending on how hard you are exercising.

BASIC PRINCIPLES

It doesn't matter whether you are a wrestler, a swimmer or a volleyball player; five training principles dictate the amount of improvement you will make in your strength and conditioning efforts. These are *overload, specificity, progression, recuperation,* and *reversibility.* Understanding each of these is important to developing training programs that will work.

Overload without Overtraining

Perhaps you have heard the expression, "Whatever doesn't kill us makes us stronger." That basically sums up overload. To describe how overload really works, we should add to the phrase, "Whatever doesn't kill us OR injure us OR overtrain us makes us stronger." Overload means that, when you increase how hard or how long you train, your body undergoes a training adaptation and becomes stronger or more capable of performing longer workouts. This is the foundation of conditioning improvement and strength development.

Overload in the weight room means lifting to your maximum capability. You do as many repetitions as you can with whatever resistance you are using, and then, after a short rest you do it again. An example of endurance overload would be to add five minutes to your usual training run. The remaining training principles will help you understand what kinds of overload to use and how often to use it.

Specificity

Effective overload is designed to target your specific needs. Specificity means your training adaptation depends on the kind of exercise you do. In other words, you should focus your training in ways that are as similar to wrestling as possible. This becomes more important as you get closer to your competition. There are two types of specificity important for wrestlers.

Intensity specificity means you train as hard in a workout as you will in competition. This is the reason that coaches probably have you running sprints as part of wrestling practice instead of running long distances like a three-mile run. To achieve **movement specificity** you should include exercises that have body movements similar to how you move in a match. Wrestling is the best way to do this, but a variety of other training type activities, called cross-training, can effectively supplement what you are doing in practice. Chapter two will discuss the merits of several cross-training exercises in terms of their specificity to wrestling.

Progression

Overload should be applied gradually. Experiencing a training adaptation after several weeks of hard workouts is very motivating. Therefore, some athletes are tempted to push themselves too hard in early season workouts and end up with injuries. A rule of thumb is to increase overload by no more than 10% per week. There may be situations where brief periods of planned, short-term overload can provide conditioning benefits. In a process called supercompensation your body reacts to the stresses of training by increasing strength and important cellular compounds. This is why coaches will sometimes add a hard training week within a few weeks of an important competition. However, too much overload can result in injury and overtraining syndrome.

A ten-percent-per-week increase may seem like an overly conservative approach to overload, but consider the alternative which is the increased risk of injury. For example, in the beginning of the season, coaches and wrestlers are excited to train and get into competition. Usually, wrestlers go from little or no training prior to the season to several hours of training in the first weeks of practice. As a result, many wrestling teams will have a higher percentage of their athletes with some type of injury early in the season than they will during the competition part of the season when opponents are often trying to hurt each other.

You are the only one that can reduce the risk of getting an early-season overtraining injury, because your coach may not be allowed to train you in the months leading up to the first wrestling practice. The positive side of this is that you are in total control of your conditioning and strength development, and, after reading the following chapters, you will know how to maximize your preparedness.

Recuperation

Did you ever wonder how your body gets in shape? You know that you can run to increase endurance and lift weights to get stronger, but how does exercise help you improve? After all, working out makes you tired, and the longer or harder you train, the more tired you get. The miracle of increased strength or conditioning happens after your workout. Your body responds to the stress of overload by improving the function of the various systems responsible for strength and conditioning. Adequate rest between workouts is essential to maximizing these recovery processes. Twenty-four hours is usually the minimum time required for recuperation, but it may take longer depending on the workout or the type of training. You will be able to perform certain types of exercise more often than others.

You can't just pile on extra work and expect to improve indefinitely. Any time you overload your body, it causes stress. You can recover from the right amount of stress, but too much stress over too long a time can lead to overtraining, which can cause extreme fatigue, sickness or even injury. In the best scenario, a person can recover from mild overtraining after a few days rest combined with good nutrition. In extreme cases, it can take several weeks to recover.

Reversibility

When I was about ten years old, I thought that I would be able to get my muscles strong and in shape and that I would be able to stay that way forever. I didn't understand the principle of reversibility, which is a loss of conditioning from not training often enough or hard enough. The rate of reversibility depends on the kind of shape you have achieved. Cardiovascular endurance tends to decline faster than muscular strength. Your challenge is to allow enough time to recuperate between workouts, but still train as often as necessary to increase strength and conditioning. Use the way your body feels as a guide. When you are no longer sore or tired from previous workouts then you have achieved supercompensation and are ready perform your next workout for that mode of training.

Summary of the Training Principles

These training principles are the foundation to your strength and conditioning program. You will read about how these principles are put into action in the following chapters. Applying the principles can be easier by using the FITT principle.

GET FITT

The concept of FITT has been around for years, but it is still the best way to organize your training. The letters stand for *frequency, intensity, time,* and *type,* respectively. These principles are interdependent; the application of each one depends on the others.

Frequency

Frequency refers to how often you train and applies the recuperation and reversibility principles. Harder workouts will require greater recuperation, so you must allow more time for recovery between workouts to avoid overtraining. Easier workouts require greater frequency to maintain conditioning and avoid reversibility. The training frequency required for developing skills is greater than for maintaining skills. When you first learn a skill, frequent practices are necessary, perhaps daily or even several times a day. Once you have become competent, you can maintain your edge with less frequent practice sessions.

Intensity

Intensity is a measure of how hard you train. This is an application of the overload principle. Training intensities are usually estimated relative to your maximum ability. For aerobic endurance training, like running, for example, intensity is relative to your estimated maximum heart rate. Strength training intensities are generally percentages of a weight lifting maximum. Once you have established a desired level of conditioning or strength, intensity becomes more important than frequency in terms of maintenance. In other words, you will be able to slightly decrease your frequency and still maintain your conditioning, if your workouts are intense enough.

Time

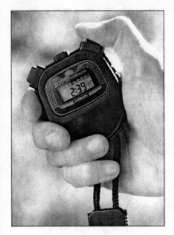

Time, another application of the overload principle, refers to the duration of your workout. Increasing the duration of a workout or even a part of the workout, like a running interval, for example, increases the overload and causes greater endurance or strength. Usually the duration of a workout is inversely related to the intensity. The harder you workout the less time you can sustain the intensity and vice versa.

Type

The type of exercises you select should be as specific to wrestling as possible in terms of the movement patterns. Obviously, this is challenging because of the complexity of movements in wrestling. In the upcoming chapters, you will learn some of the best strength and conditioning exercises in terms of their carryover benefit for you as a wrestler.

MUSCLE FIBERS AND PERFORMANCE

Do you have a preference for one kind of exercise intensity over another? Perhaps you are naturally fast sprinter, but you hate to run long distances. On the other hand, maybe endurance is your thing, but you don't seem to make improvements on your strength as fast as other people. Generally, most people tend to have natural strength and explosiveness or they are better suited to endurance activities. Your natural abilities are related to the performance properties of your muscles.

Hundreds of skeletal muscles in our bodies work in groups to make thousands of movements possible. They must be able to exert force (strength) and sustain that force (endurance). Muscle cells, which are also called fibers, have special properties that allow them to possess varying amounts of strength or endurance.

Fibers with the highest potential for strength are able to contract quickly and with a great amounts of tension; these are called fast-twitch fibers. Slow-twitch fibers, on the other hand, have tremendous potential for endurance. Intermediate fibers are fast-twitch fibers which, through training, have adapted to have greater endurance capacity. This doesn't mean there are only three distinct muscle fiber types. It's probably more accurate to say that there is a range of strength and endurance characteristics muscle fibers possess. Training can influence some of these characteristics.

Each of the muscles in a person's body has both fast-twitch and slow-twitch fibers. The proportion of fast- to slow-twitch fibers depends on the function of the muscle. For example, your neck muscles hold up your head while you are awake. These muscles are so resistant to fatigue that you don't even need to think about it. Your postural muscles work the same way. Slow-twitch fibers that can maintain muscle tension carry much of this load, so your neck and your postural muscles rely more on slow-twitch muscle fibers. On the other hand, your leg muscles carry the load for your entire body. They must be able to generate force rapidly such as when you are exploding off the bottom position while executing an escape. Thus, fast-twitch fibers are important in your lower body.

People differ in terms of their individual proportions of fast- or slow-twitch fibers. Someone with more fast-twitch fibers will be stronger and more powerful than a person who has a higher proportion of slow-twitch fibers. However, the person with more slow-twitch fibers will have an easier time developing endurance. The proportion of fast-twitch to slow-twitch fibers a person has is genetically determined.

Exercise scientists have methods that enable them to count the numbers of each type of muscle fiber and determine if a person has predominantly fast- or slow-twitch fibers. However, this is usually done to determine how exercise programs influence changes in muscle fiber type. You can determine whether you tend to have more fast- or slow-twitch fibers simply by how you perform in various activities.

If you are a person who is consistently good at things that require power and speed, such as a vertical jump or a 40-yard dash, but find it a little harder to be a distance runner, then you probably have more fast-twitch fibers. On the other hand, if you have naturally good endurance, but struggle, even with training, to run a fast 40-yard dash, then you most likely possess more slow-twitch fibers.

Wrestling requires you to be able to exert a lot of force quickly, but also sustain a high level of that force for several minutes, so it is important to train your fast-twitch fibers to be fatigue resistant. Your body uses various energy systems to do this.

ENERGY SYSTEMS

Energy is the ability to do work. It allows you to breathe, enables you to run, and to stay awake while you are reading this book. Most importantly, energy is what makes your muscles contract. A little molecule called ATP is really what provides the energy for muscle contraction. The food we eat and the air we breathe benefit our ability to make ATP. Your body is constantly breaking down and rebuilding ATP.

When ATP breaks down, it releases energy, but your body must regenerate this ATP for continued activity. This occurs through a combination of three energy systems: the phosphagen system, the glycolytic system, and the aerobic system. Intensity influences how fast you need to regenerate ATP and is the primary factor determining which system provides the most energy at any given time.

High-intensity exercises are usually performed with effort that you cannot sustain very long. A 40-yard dash, for example, would be considered high intensity, because of the high forces your muscles are experiencing and the demand for rapid production of ATP. On the other hand, running a mile is lower intensity—even if you are running as fast as possible for that distance, because you cannot sustain the pace of your fastest 40-yard dash for a mile. This is also true with wrestling efforts, so it is important that you don't confuse intensity with effort. You can give full effort to a thirty-minute practice match, but the pace and intensity will not be as high as your best 6- or 7-minute match.

Intensity is very important for training purposes because of the need for specificity in training. At lower intensities, the oxygen system provides most of the energy, but at high intensities, like wrestling, the ATP-PC and lactic acid systems provide the energy. You must train at the intensity you want to compete to develop the conditioning, timing and skills in ways most similar to competition; therefore, you should focus on developing the ATP-PC and lactic acid systems.

ATP-PC System

I think of the ATP-PC system as an explosive 112-pound wrestler. It's a fast reaction that drives activities that require short bursts of energy, usually lasting about six seconds or less, such as a stand-up, a 40-yard dash, or a maximal weight lifting attempt.

Chemical reactions that allow this are so fast that they don't need oxygen—they are *anaerobic*. In other words, you don't have to start breathing harder before you run your first sprint of a workout. Because oxygen is not necessary, the ATP-PC system is active at the start of all exercise. Full-effort sprints that are less than 10 seconds would maximize the development of the ATP-PC system, but such short sprints wouldn't benefit you in wrestling. You need to go longer, so you must train the lactic acid system, which is kind of a bummer, because lactic acid system training is the hardest training on the planet!

Lactic Acid System

Remember the last time you felt your muscles burning while you were wrestling. Was it yesterday? Or was it last week? It was most likely that last time you wrestled and you probably feel it every time you wrestle. You feel this way due to an accumulation of lactic acid in the muscles.

Scientists call the lactic acid system the *glycolytic* system because it involves the breakdown of sugars. The proper term of this energy system is glycolysis. "Glyco" refers to carbohydrate (sugar) and "lysis" means to break something down. I prefer calling it the lactic acid system, because it brings back the not-so-pleasant memories of what I felt when I was training to develop the system. If you have ever done sprints with short rest periods, you can probably relate.

Lactic Acid and Soreness

Some people mistakenly suggest that lactic acid accumulation is the cause of muscle soreness. If this were true, then every time you increased lactic acid, you would be sore. Most of the soreness you feel in the days after a workout is probably more related to small injuries to structural tissue in the muscle fibers.

Interval training, which involves several sprint intervals, separated by periods of rest, is the best way to improve your ability to perform in spite of high accumulations of lactic acid. In chapter two you will learn how to use interval training to maximize your conditioning and toughness.

WORK HARD, WORK SMART

At the highest levels of wrestling competition everyone works hard. The key to winning is to work smart. Understanding the training essentials in this chapter will help you make the right decisions. Actually, these training essentials are not confined to wrestling. They apply to whatever exercise goal that you have. In the upcoming chapters you see examples of workouts that apply these principles. However, you should not limit yourself to just the workouts listed. Using correct training principles and creativity, you can develop your own workouts to take your training to a new level. Let's get started!

RECOMMENDED READING

Baechle, T.R., R.W. Earle, and D. Wathen. Resistance training. In: *Essentials of Strength Training and Conditioning*, 3rd ed. T.R. Baechle ed. Champaign, IL: Human Kinetics. 2008.

Gambetta, V. *Athletic Development: The Art and Science of Functional Sports Conditioning*. Champaign, IL: Human Kinetics. 2007.

Powers, S.K. and S.L. Dodd. *Total Fitness and Wellness*, 3rd ed. San Francisco, CA: Pearson, Benjamin Cummings. 2009.

Wilmore, J.H. and D.L. Costill. *Physiology of Exercise and Sport*. Champaign, IL: Human Kinetics. 1994.

CHAPTER 2

FITT to Wrestle

Technique wins the first period. Conditioning wins the second period. Guts win the third period.

-J. Robinson, 2001 NCAA Coach of the Year

CROSS TRAINING

If a wrestling match is only six or seven minutes long, and you have hard practices for two hours a day, is it really necessary to condition or lift weights (cross train) in addition to wrestling practice? The answer is YES! And there are several good reasons for this.

First of all, cross training reduces the risk of overuse injuries. Wrestling specifically develops movements in certain directions and at specific speeds, but it fails to develop other movement patterns. This imbalance in training can create strength or flexibility imbalances, which can increase injuries.

When you think about it, you will realize that good, offensive wrestling keeps your joints in a protected, limited range of motion. Your shoulders, for example, don't go through the full range of motion until someone starts cranking on them. In that situation, your opponent helps you discover ranges of motion that you did not know existed! Cross training strengthens joints to reduce injuries.

A second reason to cross train is that you can be in total control of the intensity of the workout. Wrestling does not offer this flexibility. You are typically limited by the skill and conditioning level of your opponent and may not be pushed sufficiently by less skilled practice partners. Coaches try to accommodate for this by setting up drills where several partners rotate on a single wrestler. Nevertheless, this does not always result in a very skilled wrestler being pushed to the limit, nor should you wait for a coach to create this opportunity for you.

Cross training can be mentally refreshing. Such a workout can condition your body and allow you to track your conditioning improvement. After your initial improvement in your conditioning (usually in the early season), you will find that you feel better in practice. Afterwards, it will be difficult to judge your improvement by how you feel. When I was competing, I could recognize that I was able to do more things when I was tired and that my recovery seemed better. However, I was able to measure my conditioning and strength improvements through cross training activities.

Probably the best reason to cross train is that it builds mental toughness and is a personal affirmation of how badly you want to achieve your goals. I cannot stress this value enough. My experiences as a coach have led me to believe that athletes who condition themselves are in better shape, even if they do the same amount of work as someone that must be pushed to condition.

How often should you do off-the-mat conditioning workouts? How hard should they be? How long should they last? What kinds of exercises should you do? There are so many variables to consider that it is little wonder that we sometimes stick to the same workout with little variation or do nothing for fear of making a training error. Fortunately, there is an easy way to design your own conditioning program and effectively include all the necessary components.

Programming each of these variables depends on several factors including the time of year in question and your conditioning strengths and weaknesses. Outstanding athletes are skilled at focusing on the right training priorities at the right time. These athletes separate themselves from others by improving upon their weaknesses while maintaining their strengths. Using the FITT principle introduced in chapter one will help you organize your training to maximize your results.

FREQUENCY

Elite athletes commit to some type of training most days of the week throughout the year. This does not mean that every athlete should train this often. Training frequency depends on several factors including your level of training, how hard you are training and the time of year.

Training Level

Your training level is based on the number of years you have been actively training and your level of conditioning at a given time. If you are untrained (have not trained extensively) or out of shape, then three training days per week with a day of rest in between is a good starting point. If you have previously trained, then you should be able to progress to training five or six days per week rather quickly. Here are two progression schemes you can use depending on whether you are untrained or just out of shape.

Frequency for an Untrained Wrestler	
Weeks	**Training Days/Intensity**
1 - 2	Monday-easy; Wednesday-easy/moderate; Friday-easy
3 - 4	Monday-moderate; Wednesday-easy; Friday-moderate
5 - 6	Monday-hard; Tuesday-easy; Thursday-moderate; Friday-easy
7 - 8	Monday-hard; Tuesday-easy; Thursday-hard; Friday-easy
9	Begin five or six days per week alternating hard and easy days

Frequency for an out-of-shape Wrestler	
Weeks	Training Days/Intensity
1	Monday, Wednesday, Friday-easy to moderate
2	Monday-moderate; Wednesday-easy, Friday-moderate
3	Monday-hard; Tuesday-easy; Thursday-Moderate; Friday-easy
4	Monday-hard; Tuesday easy; Thursday-hard; Friday-easy
5	Begin five or six days per week alternating hard and easy days

These frequency recommendations factor in all your training activities, not just things you do in addition to wrestling practice. If you have not trained extensively in the off-season and begin five-day practice weeks, then you should avoid doing extra conditioning workouts in the first few weeks. Your body will be under enough stress with the increased training load and you are likely to do more harm than good by adding extra workouts.

When I coached, I followed the example of my own college coaches who used progression models similar to the ones you just saw. College coaches generally have the freedom to work with athletes several weeks before any competitions begin. However, high school teams may only have a few weeks of practice before the season's first dual meet or tournament, so you may not have the luxury of a more gradual progression. You should do everything possible to enter the first wrestling practice in shape.

Time of Year

During the off-season, your primary focus should be on improving upon your weaknesses. You should invest a minimum of two or three days per week doing this. A commitment to two workouts per week is possible even though you might have other activities in the off-season. You may be surprised how much such a minimum time investment can help you. Even two workouts per week over an eight-month period will add up to over 60 workouts! What makes this even more of an advantage to you is that many of your opponents are not doing this.

Here is an example of a three-day week of strength and conditioning program that can be completed in about an hour.

Off-season Strength and Conditioning					
Monday	Tuesday	Wednesday	Thursday	Friday	Sat/Sun
Hard lift 50 min. Sprints 10 min.	OFF	Lift 80% Monday's load Sprints 15 min.	OFF	Lift 90% Monday's load Sprints 10 min.	OFF

During wrestling season, you will likely spend 15 hours or more each week practicing wrestling or competing. Any additional training you do is to support your wrestling training. The heavy training demands of wrestling practice decrease the need for a lot of extra conditioning activities. In the following example, the lifting sessions are short compared to what they might be in the off-season, and there are only two days of sprints, which may be part of your wrestling practice.

In-season Strength and Conditioning					
Monday	Tuesday	Wednesday	Thursday	Friday	Sat/Sun
Hard lift 30 min.	Sprints 10 min. after practice	Lift 80% Monday's load	Sprints 10 min. after practice	No extra work	Sat. - Compete Sun. - OFF

Frequency also depends on the amount of time you need between each workout. High-intensity workouts like sprinting or weight lifting create forces significant enough to damage structures in the muscle tissues. Usually this damage is minimal. In fact, the damage is an important stimulus to induce muscle remodeling, which is how the body replaces damaged tissue with stronger tissue. Resting between workouts is essential to the remodeling process. You should plan on resting a minimum of 48 hours between high-intensity workouts. This does not mean that you cannot workout during the 48-hour period; it does mean that you should not directly stress that same body part in the same way. Thus, you might stress your entire body with hard wrestling one day and come back the next day with heavy lifting.

INTENSITY

Measuring workout intensity for cardiovascular training has many advantages. Two important benefits are monitoring your progress and reducing the risk of overtraining. When you know the intensity at which you can do something, you are able to gauge your performance regardless of how you might feel during the workout. You can also measure your progress by how your recovery ability improves over time for a given intensity.

There are many ways to describe intensity. For weight training, it is measured as a percentage of a one-repetition maximum. Cardiovascular work is measured as a percentage of your maximum heart rate which is estimated to be 220 minus a person's age. However, wrestling requires work at your maximum intensity as much as possible, so it's impractical to use heart rate to measure your intensity. My preference is to use words like "hard," "medium," and "easy" to describe the quality of the effort from a performance perspective. These words take into consideration both the intensity relative to your maximum and the overall amount of work you do.

For example, you could run a 100-yard sprint at maximal intensity, but, if you only did one sprint, the overall workout wouldn't be very hard. "Hard" is considered to be 100% of your physical and mental effort; "medium" intensity is 90%, and "easy" is about 80%.

There is little point in performing cardiovascular training below the level you need to exert in a match. Every conditioning workout should involve sprints at 100% of how hard you can go. You can alternate hard, easy and medium days by manipulating the duration of each sprint or how many you use. For off-season training I like to do hard days on Monday, easy days on Wednesdays and Moderate days on Friday. These sprints are usually shorter in duration than in-season training, because your conditioning levels don't need to be as high and it is nice to have a change of pace now and then. Here is an example of a week of conditioning you could do in the off-season.

Off-season Strength Conditioning Intensities					
Monday	Tuesday	Wednesday	Thursday	Friday	Sat/Sun
Hard day Sprints 20-30 sec. each 10-12 reps	OFF	**Easy Day** Sprints 20-30 sec. each 5-7 reps	OFF	**Medium Day** Sprints 20-30 sec. each 8-10 reps	OFF

During the season, the days you pick to be hard, medium and easy days will depend mostly on when you have competitions. I recommend at least two days recovery from a hard day of anything before competing.

TIME: HOW LONG SHOULD YOU WORKOUT?

At this point you can probably see a trend happening in the FITT principle. Frequency was based on intensity, and intensity was based on the time (duration) of a sprint. You should consider the time of each sprint, the length of recovery between sprints, as well as the overall duration of your workouts.

Sprint Duration

In chapter one, you learned about the energy systems. Most of the energy used in a wrestling match comes from the lactic acid system, which becomes very important after about 20 seconds of all-out effort. Usually the lactic acid system cannot maintain intensities much longer than a minute or two. Most of your sprints should be somewhere between 30 seconds and two minutes.

Longer sprints are not necessarily better, because your intensity will drop. Besides, with wrestling periods being two minutes long, and the fact that they are interrupted at various times (such as going off the mat), you rarely need to be at 100% intensity for the full two minutes. Thus, in your training it is better to go harder than longer. I found that working up to one-minute sprints was effective for me.

Between-sprint recovery for lactic acid system training should be about 2-3 times the duration of the sprint. This can be manipulated depending on the length of the sprint and your ability to recover. For example, a short sprint of 20 seconds at an all-out effort when you are beginning interval training may require a full minute of recovery. However, if you are doing a two minute sprint, then a full six minutes of recovery may not be practical in terms of the length of the overall workout.

Some of your recovery depends on your muscle fiber type as well. I've had athletes who had tremendous low-intensity endurance, but couldn't produce much power. These guys could sprint hard for a minute, and they would be fully recovered after a minute. On the other hand, I've seen powerful athletes that struggled to go all-out for a minute, even after several weeks of training, and could not recover in three minutes. The key is to find an interval duration that will require intense physical effort and mental concentration. If your intensity drops by more than 10% (measured by power output, rpm, etc. on a digital display or distance sprinted), then decrease the duration of the sprint.

It is also possible to have several different sprint durations in the same workout. The sprint intervals in the 40-minute running workout below all tax the ATP-PC and lactic acid systems, but the various durations of each sprint keep it interesting and make it a good workout to use when you are getting into shape. I liked to use the running workouts below in the pre-season when I was transitioning from off-season to prepare for upcoming wrestling practices. You can do these workouts on a track or on trails. Do the interval running workout early in the training week (Monday or Tuesday), give yourself about 48 hours rest and do the match-length interval running on Thursday or Friday.

Running Workout (40 minutes)	Match-Length Interval Running
1. 5-minute warm-up (light jog progressing to faster running)	1. 5-minute warm-up
2. Five 5-second sprints, 15 sec. rest	2. 3 one-mile* runs as fast as possible with a three-minute rest
3. Four 20-second sprints, 60 sec. rest	3. 10-minute cool down
4. Three 40-second sprints, 120 sec. rest	
5. 15-minute cool down (light jog and stretching)	*Large athletes (>150 pounds) or slower athletes could perform ¾-mile runs. The goal is to finish the first run in the time it takes to wrestle a match (~6-7 minutes).

Although the match-length intervals draw more on the oxygen system, it is a good workout to get you ready for hard practices early in the season. Regardless of your running speed, you should be able to finish it in about 30-40 minutes.

At the end of the season, when you are preparing for state or nationals, you should keep the intensity high, but reduce the number of intervals you do over a few weeks. Tapering the volume will allow you to maintain conditioning but increase your body's energy stores. This is my favorite peaking workout.

Peaking Interval Training (PIT)				
Week	**Work**	**Rest**	**Reps**	**Effort**
1-2	:30	:90	12	100%
3-4	:45	2:15	10	100%
5-6	1:00	3:00	7	100%
7-8	1:00	3:00	4	100%

Do this twice per week starting eight weeks before your state or national qualifying tournament. Notice that the rest period is three times longer than work interval. This concerns some people who feel that the rest period should be shortened as the program progresses. Shortening the rest periods is an option, but this should only be done if you can maintain intensity.

Another option might include foregoing the 30-second work intervals in weeks 1 and 2, if they are too easy. In this case, your program would start with two weeks at 45-second intervals followed by six weeks at one-minute intervals. In the final two weeks you might also decrease the rest interval to two-and-a-half minutes or two minutes, if you can maintain sprint intensity. The last two weeks the volume of work is decreased to four repetitions to maximize your recovery while maintaining intensity.

An excellent alternative to using running as the mode of exercise for the Peaking Interval Training workouts would be to cycle on a Schwinn Air Dyne or to use a commercial-grade elliptical trainer. This will reduce the potential for impact-related injuries. Just set the resistance so the speed you are moving your arms and legs is similar to hard running and the resistance is such that at the end of the interval you feel like you just ran a hard lap on a quarter-mile track.

Interval training on the Schwinn Air Dyne has excellent carryover to wrestling.

TYPE OF WORKOUTS: BEST MODES OF CONDITIONING FOR WRESTLERS

Wrestling involves all of your muscles; some muscles may be working dynamically by continually lengthening and shortening and some are working isometrically when you are squeezing an opponent or holding your own position. To maximize the metabolic specificity of the workout, you should use exercises that activate as many muscles as possible. This not only conditions the muscles, but it also burns more calories and helps maintain a lean body composition.

It is challenging to find one exercise that will provide all the movements that are similar to wrestling. You may have also noticed that you can be in shape to do one kind of activity, but not another. If all you do is running, for example, you get to a point where you hit a plateau. Using different modes of training will require constant adaptation and mental effort to work hard, which carries over to wrestling. Variety will also reduce the risk of overuse injuries. Three common cross training exercises are running, swimming and cycling. Each has advantages and disadvantages.

Running

For convenience, there is no better exercise than running. You need no equipment other than a decent pair of running shoes and some kind of clothing. I like the fact that you carry your own body weight when you run. Postural muscles are activated. You must lift your own legs and drive with your arms. All these benefits transfer in valuable ways to wrestling.

Running has limitations as well. First, your joints take a pounding that you may not realize during the workout. In fact, the toll that running can have on your joints may not be felt until months or years down the road. This is one reason that you should try to run on shock-absorbing surfaces as much as possible. Avoid surfaces like pavement and try to run more on gravel, grass or dirt trails. If you opt for trail running, take safety precautions such as knowing where you are going and telling someone when to expect your return.

Another limitation is that running is not very specific to wrestling. Good wrestling position is a compact body with flexed knees and hips and other joints. Efficient running, on the other hand, is relaxed and extended. For that reason, your running should be limited to hard running and sprints as opposed to distance running.

Biking

Biking is more specific to wrestling than running from a total-body perspective. Your hip and knee angles are similar to the positions your legs are in when you are in your stance. Even your elbows may be close to your body depending on the type of bike you ride and the adjustments you've made to your seat and handlebars. The constant tension on the quadriceps muscles of your thighs is very similar to what you feel in a match.

Another advantage of biking is that it tends to be easier on the joints than running. There is less of the pounding impact associated with running, unless you are like me and you wreck a lot. Always wear a helmet and obey traffic laws!

Obviously, you need some type of a bike to use this as a conditioning activity. This can be a stationary bike or a regular one. You should not invest a tremendous amount of money in a bike you will use for conditioning. There are many fancy models available to help you go faster with less energy, but your goal is to work hard. Don't get too carried away in the purchase of your clothing either (with the exception of a well constructed helmet). In cooler weather you can bundle up in heavy sweats that are not the least bit aerodynamic, but actually catch the wind like a sail and make you work harder. Another advantage of low-budget clothing is that it will make you feel old school. Remember the sweats that Rocky Balboa wore in the first couple of Rocky flicks? You don't have to swallow the raw eggs, however.

I discovered the advantages of biking by accident. My bikes have all been low-end mountain bikes, which I rode for transportation, not necessarily for conditioning. One year my commute was about 12 miles round trip, which was about 20-30 minutes each way. Mid-way through one season, I realized that biking was improving my takedown wrestling. Previously, I had been chronically coming out of my stance and giving opponents easy shots. Even worse, I was not very good at grinding to finish a takedown when an opponent stopped my initial momentum. Biking helped me to stay in a good stance and it strengthened my legs specifically in the movement I needed to finish the tough shots.

Swimming

Many people believe that swimming is the best form of exercise. Although the movements are not identical to wrestling movements, swimming may provide enough other benefits to make it the best form of cross training a wrestler can perform. For one thing, it is excellent cardio and the water creates tremendous resistance, which will develop your muscular endurance as well as your cardiovascular system.

When I coached, I tried to get the team in the pool as often as possible, but especially at the end of the season. Most of the wrestlers on my teams were not naturally gifted swimmers, which made the workouts even more challenging. Typically, we would perform the peaking interval workout (page 38) twice a week for our early morning conditioning. I would tie an elastic band around their waists and tether it to one end of the pool. The wrestlers would try to swim to the other end against the resistance of the band. The harder they tried to swim, the less efficient they tended to be and the harder the sprint became. The workout would last about 30 minutes and it was impossible for anyone to cheat.

Unfortunately, swimming is an underutilized mode of conditioning for obvious reasons, such as the lack of pool availability. Nevertheless, I believe it is the best form of cross training for reducing the risk of injuries and conditioning without further beating up your body. Swimming is easier on your joints than compared to running, and it works numerous muscles simultaneously. Swimming will maintain the ranges of motion in joints and other areas of your body in ways that wrestling does not.

Many wrestlers have inflexible shoulders. In some cases, injuries have contributed to the lack of flexibility, but often wrestling practices train the anterior, or front, part of the shoulder more than the back. (Think of the how many push-ups and pummeling drills you have done in practices compared to the number of exercises designed to strengthen the pulling muscles of your shoulder.) Swimming strengthens your shoulder through the entire range of motion in a way that you cannot duplicate in the weight room. Such strengthening may reduce the likelihood of getting a shoulder injury. You should note, however, that swimming will likely aggravate an existing shoulder injury.

Swimming can also provide tremendous benefits to your lower back health. I learned this first-hand after a low-back injury. Coincidentally, I enrolled in a college swim class soon after the injury. Despite the fact that I felt like a concrete truck in the water, I stuck with it because it was about the only workout I could do with my injury. I was amazed at the improvement in the muscles around the injury. Several of the swimming strokes almost perfectly matched the movements prescribed by my physical therapist. Specifically, the swimming helped me to strengthen the rotary muscles of the trunk responsible for allowing side-to-side twisting movements. This had a tremendous benefit of reducing the chronic tension and pain in that area.

I've been an advocate of swimming as a mode of injury prevention since then. If you are fortunate enough to have access to a pool, challenge yourself to add swimming to your cross-training activities. Never swim without the supervision of a trained lifeguard and avoid any kind of horseplay that would not contribute to the training benefit.

The same work-to-rest ratio applies for swimming as any other conditioning. Here is my favorite swim workout:

*Select distances based on how far you can swim in 30 seconds or one minute.

Lactic Acid System Swimming

1. Warm-up 100 yards easy
2. 4 x 25-yard* sprints with one-minute rest (about 1:2 work:rest ratio)
3. 4 x 50-yard sprints with a 3 minute rest (1:3 ratio)
4. Cool down: tread water 5 minutes

The Super Circuit

While running, biking, and swimming have a well-established place as cross-training activities, exercise equipment like stair steppers, elliptical trainers and other devices are excellent modes of training. Display screens on these devices provide information such as power output, distance traveled, calories burned and others.

One of my favorite workouts, the super circuit, involves the use of an ergometer (my favorite is an elliptical trainer) and weights. I alternate weight training sets of 8-12 repetitions as heavy as possible with one-minute intervals of cardio training at near maximal intensity. The elliptical trainer allows me to see how fast I am moving and the display challenges me to keep my power output high when I get tired. I like the super circuit as an alternative to traditional weight training.

If you were to time a person's activity in the weight room, you would most likely observe that the majority of the workout time is spent resting between lifting sets. Although rest is important when training with heavy weights, conditioning for wrestling is more dependent on developing strength-endurance. I like to add hard cardio exercise between my sets. The following workout takes about 30 minutes:

Super Circuit

Warm-up: five minutes on elliptical at moderate intensity

Cardio intervals: One-minute sprints at 90 % effort between lifting sets

Strength intervals: 8-12 reps heavy as possible

- Leg Press
- Chest Press
- Leg Curl
- Seated Cable Row
- Leg Extension

- Shoulder Press
- Lat Pull Down
- Arm Curl
- Triceps Extension
- Abdominal Crunch

Cool-down: five minutes walking and light stretching

You can modify this workout by doing all the upper- and lower-body exercises together or by doing multiple sets of specific exercises like a strength workout. Refer to the appendix for several different super circuit workouts to help you progress in training. Although the super circuit uses weights, it is not necessarily the best way to build absolute strength. If you are already in shape, it won't do much to increase your one-rep max on anything, because you are not lifting above a critical threshold for strength development. However, the workout will make you feel just like you do in a match, where your muscles need to contract with a moderate percentage of max strength while you are tired and breathing hard.

PEAK WHEN IT COUNTS

The quote at the beginning of this chapter is true. Matches are won and lost in the second and third periods. If you can commit to follow the workout on page 46 for nine weeks, you will not only be in shape to dominate your opponents, but you will develop a mental toughness so critical to success at the highest levels of wrestling. The following program utilizes the Peaking Interval Training (PIT) workout and will enable you to maximize your endurance strength and allow you to taper and have increased energy when it counts.

RECOMMENDED READING

Horswill, C.A. Interval training for wrestlers. *Wrestling USA* September, 1992.

Kell, R. The use of interval training to condition for wrestling. *Strength and Conditioning*. October, 1997.

| \multicolumn{4}{c}{**Peaking Interval Training (PIT)**} |
Weeks	Competition Activities	Monday*	Thursday
1-2	Duals/tourneys	PIT Weeks 1-2 Mode: Swim or Bike	Super circuit† 30 minutes
3-4	Duals/tourneys	PIT Weeks 3-4 Mode: Swim or Bike	Super circuit 30 minutes
5-6	Duals/tourneys	PIT Weeks 5-6 Mode: Swim or Bike	Super circuit 30 minutes
7	No competition‡	Four intervals of PIT Mode: Swim or Bike	Super circuit 20 minutes
8	Qualifying tourney	Four intervals of PIT	No workout
9	State/national tournament	Four intervals of PIT	No workout

*Training days should be adjusted to accommodate competitions.

†Use a variety of strength exercises or a choose from the workouts in the appendix

‡Competition activities in weeks 7 and 8 might be switched.

CHAPTER 3

Got Strength?
Safety and Technique

SAFETY

Strength training is a rewarding and enjoyable activity, but it does carry a risk for injuries. Therefore, safety is the most important principle of strength training. Many people think that strength training is just about increasing your performance, but an often-overlooked reason is to reduce the risk of getting injured while you are wrestling. Attending to the following areas will help you avoid the most common weight room injuries and safely develop your strength:

- Obtain medical clearance and do exercises appropriate for your development and skill level
- Include a proper warm-up and cool down
- Avoid horseplay
- Use safe equipment and wear proper attire
- Have an attentive lifting partner and use correct lifting technique

Medical Clearance and Appropriate Exercises

If you've read exercise books or watched an exercise video, there is generally a statement that says something like, "Before engaging in an exercise program, you should consult a physician…" Not to be outdone by anyone else, I will tell you the same thing.

Having medical clearance is especially important in strength training for two reasons. One reason is to make sure your heart doesn't have any irregularities that could be a problem during your workout. Many people think that only aerobic exercise stresses your heart. However, during heavy strength training exercises, the tension on your muscles and other factors can significantly increase the pressure on your arteries (your blood pressure), which means the heart must work much harder.

A licensed health care provider can also help you identify if your body is physically mature enough to perform traditional weight training exercises without risking injury. He or she will likely ask you some questions and give you a physical examination.

Let's be frank. You and I both know that one of the things the "doc" will want to figure out is whether you've hit puberty, which is one sign that you can perform exercises like squats and power cleans without risking injury to your growth plates. Another advantage of having reached puberty is that is a sign that your body is producing growth hormones at an increased level, which will accelerate your training results.

This isn't to say that a person cannot strength train before puberty. In fact, exercise scientists now believe that the risks of children lifting weights are lower than originally thought. This makes sense when you consider all the farm kids that routinely lift heavy loads from a young age and yet grow to a normal stature. Most of the concern revolves around potential injuries to the growth plate, which can cause premature closing of this area on a bone and stunt a person's growth. In reality, the forces upon your

bones are much greater during sport participation than they are with most weight lifting exercises. Therefore, a well-structured program based on the following guidelines will reduce these risks. Also remember that you can effectively develop strength with body-weight exercises such as pull-ups, push-ups, rope climbing and others.

If you haven't hit puberty, but you still want to do traditional weight training exercises, use a weight that you can safely lift 10 or 12 times as opposed to one that you can only lift once or twice. You can even perform total-body exercises like the squat or power clean as long as the load is light.

Warming-up and Cooling Down

All your workouts should begin with a thorough warm-up, which will increase blood flow to your skeletal muscles, and prepare the connective tissue in your joints for the stresses you will place upon them. Warm-ups that include aerobic exercise will have the added benefit of increasing your alertness and general state of arousal, which can enhance your workout.

A comprehensive warm-up will include five to ten minutes of general aerobic exercises such as jogging or cycling followed by several minutes of exercises that are more specific to the movements in your workout. I also like to include some gymnastic and agility exercises into my warm-up to develop core musculature, agility and balance.

Traditionally, people have performed static stretching (where you stretch and hold the position) in a warm-up to reduce the risk of injury. However, static stretching has not been proven to reduce injuries. On the other hand, it does not increase the risk of injury either. Probably the best flexibility activities to use in a warm-up would be dynamic, range-of-motion exercises, such as arm rotations and trunk rotations. This will "loosen up" the areas you target and add a small strength stimulus in ways not possible with traditional weight room exercises.

TRUNK ROTATIONS: Perform this exercise by rotating forward, to both sides, and backward. Extend the reach throughout the hands.

DYNAMIC TOE TOUCHES AND OVERHEAD REACH: Bend forward to touch the toes then reach overhead as shown above.

Here is a total body warm-up routine:

1. Ten minutes of cardiovascular exercise (jogging, stationary bike, elliptical machine, etc.) including a three or four 10- or 15-second sprints in the last two minutes.

2. Dynamic range of motion stretches working from your trunk to your extremities:

- Trunk rotations-about eight each way
- Dynamic toe touches and overhead reaches
- Hip rotations (balance on one foot with your hands on your hips and rotating your leg in large circles with your knee bent) and arm rotations-starting with your arms adducted straight out from your body and doing several small and large, backward and forward rotations.
- Neck rotations and extremity-wrist/ankle rotations

3. Agility and gymnastic exercises

- Cartwheels (about six to each side)
- Tumbling (if there is a soft surface)
- Power skipping
- Sideways shuffling

4. A few static stretches of any areas that you feel are still a little tight

Cooling down (sometimes called warming down) is an oft-neglected but very beneficial activity. Your cool down should consist of light cardiovascular exercises to circulate the blood and keep your muscles active, which can help lower the levels of accumulated lactic acid. It will also help you reduce any light headedness that can occur if you were to go from a hard effort to complete rest. The length of your cool down depends on how hard you worked out. Continue light exercise such as jogging and walking until your breathing returns to normal and you have stopped sweating.

Muscles and connective tissues are warmest following a workout, so this would be a great time to perform static stretching, if you have areas in which you want to increase your flexibility. If you hold a static stretch for about thirty seconds and stretch that area each day, it will not be necessary to do multiple repetitions of the stretch.

Avoid Horseplay

This should be obvious, but even I have violated this safety principle at various times. Horseplay in a weight room can happen quickly. Often it occurs when one wrestler playfully grabs another and they begin jostling

HIP SOCKET ROTATIONS: While standing on one foot, take the other leg out to the side to rotate your hip socket through a full range of motion.

each other amid the exercise equipment. This can lead to injury and it distracts other athletes from their workouts.

Another type of horseplay, "maxing out" contests, occurs when athletes, who may not have a structured workout, have an impromptu lifting contest. Maxing out is not a productive activity, unless you do it at the proper time. Unsupervised max out sessions increase the potential of injury due to incorrect technique, and they take away from valuable training time. Most of your time in the weight room should be spent *developing* your strength not *demonstrating* it.

Safe Equipment and Proper Clothing

Weight rooms take a lot of abuse. Dumbbells get dropped on the floor, the cables on weight machines can become frayed after thousands of movements, and the collars used to secure weights on barbells wear out over time. This is why it is important to pay close attention to the condition of your equipment. Specifically, things to watch for include the following:

- Bent barbells, which can make them difficult to control during fast movements
- Dumbbells with loose or damaged weights that could fall off and hit you
- Frayed cables (left) or cracked cable casing on weight machines that may suddenly snap
- Dirty equipment which indicates poor maintenance and is unhealthy for your skin

Another common risk occurs when athletes fail to use collars to secure the weights when performing bench presses or squats. If collars are not readily available inform a coach or facility supervisor and use different equipment.

What you wear can also contribute to your safety. Shoes are absolutely essential in a weight room. They will help your balance, increase your traction, and provide you with at least a minimal amount of protection if a weight falls on you. There may be situations when you want exercise without the stability of your shoes to further develop your balance. This should be done in an area other than the weight room using soft weighted implements like a medicine ball.

Your choice in clothing should be based on helping you regulate your body temperature and allow for freedom of movement. Sometimes guys will remove their shirts and lift bare-chested in a public weight room. Be courteous to others and avoid doing this. Wearing a shirt will also limit the amount of skin contact you have with the bacteria-laden surfaces in a weight room.

Washing your hands during any trip you might make to the restroom is one more precaution that will benefit you and others. Hundreds of

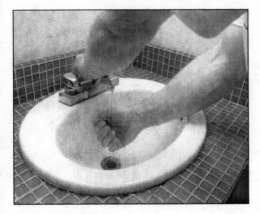 hands are placed in the exact same places in the weight room every day. These are the dirtiest places on the equipment, but they are also the least likely to be cleaned by the maintenance personnel. When was the last time you saw someone cleaning the gripping surface on a barbell, the handles on dumbbells or pull-up bars?

Spotters and Lifting Technique

A lifting partner can be a valuable asset in the weight room to "spot" you when you perform overhead lifts or attempt weights near your maximum. This person will also enable you to safely perform the strength-building repetitions at the end of a set that would be unwise without a spotter. Good lifting partners should be dedicated to safety and have the same commitment to the workout as you.

Some exercises like a squat may require more than one spotter. Set up a system of communication between everyone involved, so each person will know the amount of assistance you require during your lifts. Power exercises, such as cleans, snatches, and overhead jerks should not be spotted. Attempting to do so actually *increases* the risk of an accident. It is generally safest to drop a failed lift and step out of the way of the bar when performing power exercises.

Proper lifting technique is the most important way to ensure a productive and safe workout. Your technique will be a key factor regardless of the exercise. Four components of proper technique are posture and grip, breathing, lifting tempo, and range of motion.

Posture and Grip

Correct body posture has reference to your spine. Vertebrae and the disks that cushion them give your spinal column a curvature that should be maintained during lifting. Injuries to the disks between the lumbar vertebrae in your lower back can happen quickly, especially if your back is rounded during squats, deadlifts, or cleans. To protect this area of your back you should assume a slightly "lordotic" posture, so that your back is slightly arched as in the CORRECT photo (page 55), when your back is rounded (INCORRECT photo, page 55) you are increasing your injury risk. So keep your chest high and stick out your butt.

CORRECT: A slight arch in the back protects the vertebrae of the lower back.

INCORRECT: Rounding the lower back increases injury risk.

You can reduce the risk of dropping a weight by using a secure grip on barbells and dumbbells. The most natural grip, the closed grip, involves wrapping your fingers around the barbell and then placing your thumb across you're your first two fingers. Use a hook grip when doing power exercises like power cleans. This grip involves first wrapping your thumb around the barbell and then and locking it in place by wrapping your fingers around the bar and over your thumb.

Avoid using an open or "false grip," in which the thumb does not wrap around the barbell. Lifters will sometimes use this grip while bench pressing, but the risks outweigh any potential benefits.

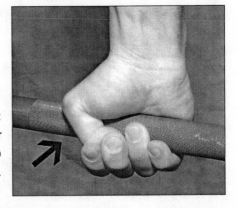

HOOK GRIP:
Use a hook grip for power cleans for greater grip strength and bar control.

Breathing

Correct breathing involves inhaling and exhaling as normally as possible during each repetition. You will find it is easier to inhale as you lower a weight and exhale as you raise a weight. Avoid holding your breath when you lift, which can cause you to tire more quickly and may leave you gasping for breath after the set. Brief periods of breath holding may naturally occur as you push through a sticking point in a range of motion, but these will probably last for less than a second.

A technique called the "Valsalva maneuver" is an advanced lifting technique used by power lifters and Olympic weight lifters when performing total-body exercises like power cleans and front squats, in which they purposely hold their breath during part of a repetition. This technique can help stabilize the torso and abdominal region, but it also has risks. Significant increases in blood pressure may occur when using the Valsalva maneuver, which puts an extra strain on the heart. Fortunately, you can develop sufficient strength for wrestling without the associated risks of intentional breath-holding techniques.

Lifting Tempo

Tempo refers to how fast you raise and lower a weight. Imagine yourself doing a biceps curl. When you raise the weight your biceps brachii shortens; this is called a *concentric* muscle action. Lengthening of this muscle when you lower the weight is called an *eccentric* muscle action. Typically, you should lower a weight slowly and under control to avoid a forceful load on the tendons at the end of a joint's range of motion.

Correct lifting tempo not only reduces injury risk, it maximizes your strength development. You may have noticed that you can lower more weight than you can lift. However, it would be impossible to effectively add weight during the eccentric phase of a repetition and then remove it during the concentric phase. You can effectively challenge your eccentric strength by going slower on the lowering phase. "Negatives" involve eccentric repetitions with heavy weight.

"Negatives"

Most people do a few negatives at the end of their last set of an exercise, usually the bench press. Negatives may also be performed as a separate workout. To properly perform a negative workout use resistance that is greater than your one-repetition maximum (1-RM) perhaps 110% or 120% of your max. Spotters are essential, and you will probably need one on each end of the barbell. You can perform two or three sets of two or three repetitions to provide an excellent overload to your muscles. Not all exercises lend themselves to negatives; you can't do them with power cleans. However, doing pull-up negatives, for example, would be an effective way to develop the upper body strength for that exercise. The overloading and eccentric muscle action disrupts muscles more than traditional concentric-eccentric lifts with lighter loads and will make your sore for several days. Therefore, use negatives sparingly, perhaps once every few weeks, and only during periods of time when your muscles are adapted to lifting high percentages of your one-repetition maximum.

Repetition tempo will vary depending on the lift or on your training goal. For example, during the weeks when you adapt yourself to a new exercise, you should perform the repetitions fairly slowly with about a one-second concentric phase and about a 1½ to two-second eccentric phase. This slower tempo will help you avoid using weights that may put too great a load on untrained connective tissue too early in the program.

Tempo can be effectively used to challenge all muscles involved in a movement. For example, when you perform a leg extension, the muscles of your upper thigh are strong enough to create enough momentum on the weight to carry it thought the range of motion. However, the muscles around your knee become more important during the last part of leg extension. If you have created too much momentum in the early part of the movement, the muscles of your knee will not be challenged as much as they would with a slower tempo. This is true for many exercises. This isn't to say that all exercises should be performed slowly. In the next chapter we will discuss when to use high-speed exercises.

Range of Motion

Always train through a joint's full range of motion. This strengthens your muscles at all potential joint angles, and reduces the risk of injury to tendons and muscles. When you reach the end of your range of motion on a squat, for example, the muscles of your lower back, hips and thighs begin to stretch, which helps slow down the bar. This helps distribute the load and reduce the force on any single joint.

MEDICINE BALL CROWN ROTATIONS: Rotate a medicine ball or a light weight around your head to strengthen your shoulders in a full range of motion.

Be careful when performing range of motion movements in a rotational manner with your shoulders. It is becoming more common for wrestlers to hold a weight in their hands and then rotate it around their heads or in other directions.

This is an excellent way to strengthen the shoulders in ways they are used in wrestling, but if abused it can lead to injury. The main problem arises when using a weight that is too heavy. Muscles of the shoulder girdle and rotator cuff are stronger in some positions than others. I made the mistake of using a weight that I could handle in one part of the range of motion but ended up injuring my rotator cuff when I rotated the weight into a different position. It's always best to err on the side of caution and use a lighter weight than your maximum for exercises that take your shoulders through a rotational range of motion.

RECOMMENDED READING

Harman, E. Biomechanics of resistance exercise. In: *Essentials of Strength Training and Conditioning*, 3rd ed. T.R. Baechle ed. Champaign, IL: Human Kinetics. 2008.

Payne, V. G. and L.D. Isaacs. *Human Motor Development: A Lifespan Approach*, 7th ed. Boston, MA: McGraw-Hill. 2002

Jeffreys, I. Warm-up and stretching. In: *Essentials of Strength Training and Conditioning*, 3rd ed. T.R. Baechle ed. Champaign, IL: Human Kinetics. 2008.

Tan, B. Manipulating resistance training program variables to optimize strength in men: A review. *Journal of Strength and Conditioning Research*, 13(3), 298-304. 1999.

CHAPTER 4
Building Up
To Take 'Em Down

Wrestling Specific Training

Of all the dimensions of performance-related fitness, strength is the king. This is the foundation for the development of speed, balance and power. It also receives the most marketing attention from individuals and companies looking to revolutionize the world with new gadgets or training devices. With all the training information bombarding us, it can be difficult to know the best way to develop the strength needed for wrestling.

Here are examples of the kinds of questions that wrestlers and parents have asked me regarding strength training:

What is the most important exercise you can do to get stronger for wrestling?

Can a wrestler get stronger without getting too big?

How many days should I strength train each week?

How long should I rest between exercises in a workout?

While these questions seem fairly straightforward, each has an answer that depends on several factors. For example, there are several exercises that are important for wrestling. The most important exercise for you may be different than that of one of your teammates because your individual weaknesses may differ. It would also depend on the time of the wrestling season.

There are numerous ways to develop strength depending on your goals. Over the next few chapters, you will learn how your body responds to strength training and how the training essentials you learned in the first chapter apply to strength training.

HOW YOUR BODY GETS STRONGER

When you overload your muscles, whether by a structured program of lifting weights or manual labor like working construction, they adapt to the extra stress by getting stronger and usually bigger. The increased strength that you notice is due to both a *neuromuscular* adaptation and a *hypertrophic* response.

Neuromuscular Adaptation

Have you ever been surprised by how quickly your ability to do a specific workout can improve? You can perform a new workout that is overwhelmingly difficult on one day, and then do the same workout a week or two later and see improvement in your ability. This essential change in your performance is the result of a neuromuscular adaptation which involves your central nervous system. Your brain sends signals down nerves that reach your muscles and control when and how hard they contract.

Imagine all the adjustments your muscles must make when you shoot a double-leg takedown. Specific muscles must contract and relax in the right order, and the muscles must establish the right amount of tension. The result of this neuromuscular activity is a well-executed and efficient move. Efficient movements are easy and don't make you as tired as uncoordinated ones. This is why we feel so much stronger or in such better shape after only a few exercise sessions. To a certain degree, the adaptation of the neuromuscular system is responsible for what people call "muscle memory," which refers to how quickly a person can get back in shape after having been in shape once before. It may also help your dad, who may not work out, to have that "old-man strength" that people talk about.

Improved neuromuscular function will benefit your wrestling ability in several ways. First of all, neuromuscular responses are specific to the kinds of movements you do. This means that the best way to get stronger at holding an opponent in a wrestling move like the cradle is to practice doing the move. You may have wrestled an opponent who did not have big muscles, but was incredibly strong. His or her neuromuscular adaptation was specific to wrestling and effectively used for leverage. A second benefit is that you can get stronger without a lot of increase in muscle size. This means your wrestling strength can improve during a season without you having to change weight classes. Last of all, neuromuscular improvements will make female wrestlers (and wrestlers who have not hit puberty) stronger, even though they don't necessarily get bigger as a result of training.

Neuromuscular improvements occur fairly rapidly and you may see noticeable changes in your strength within a few workouts, if you are just beginning to train. In fact, during the first six or eight weeks of a lifting program, improved neuromuscular function contributes more to increases in your strength than the increases in your muscle size do.

Hypertrophic Response

Hypertrophic responses mean that your muscles have gotten bigger. Increases in muscle size complement neuromuscular adaptation. When you overload your muscles, chemical messengers, called hormones, are released and act on target tissues. When anabolic (muscle building) hormones interact with muscle cells, they increase protein production which results in bigger muscles.

Muscle hypertrophy becomes important after the neuromuscular response has caused the initial increases in strength. In fact, after a few weeks of training it is usually difficult to get stronger without at least some increased muscle size. This is a great benefit if you are trying to develop a beach body, but increasing muscle mass may not be your primary goal when you are lifting during the wrestling season and need to make weight all the time.

STRENGTH TRAINING FOR WRESTLING

Functional Specificity

Muscles and joints throughout your body have different shapes and sizes based on their function, so the way you train in terms of the exercises you select, how much weight you lift and the number of repetitions ("reps') you do should reflect that. Your legs need to be strong and powerful for wrestling; therefore, you should lift heavy with relatively few reps. (You can develop the endurance you need for wrestling by wrestling.) Your arms and shoulders need to have some strength, but mostly endurance, and they need to move in a variety of directions. Therefore, when you train, you should do a variety of exercises and do a lot of reps in each set. Your back and trunk muscles need to support whatever else you are doing, so these are best developed with functional exercises such as workouts performed on a stability ball. In chapter five you will see several traditional exercises that have been made more functional in their carryover to wrestling.

Movement Specificity

When you think of the types of exercises you can do, you must consider whether they are similar to wrestling in terms of their movements and their intensities. Your choice of exercises will differ depending on whether you are trying to achieve maximal movement specificity or greater intensity (heavier weight). You might wonder how it is possible to duplicate wrestling movements in the weight room, and the reality is that you can't. Remember that neuromuscular adaptation for strength is specific to the kinds of movements you do. Therefore, you do the best you can by starting with the types of movements used in wrestling and using similar weight room exercises. Wrestling can be simplified into three important movements that can be developed in the weight room: 1) total body lifting, 2) rotational movements, and 3) pulling and squeezing. Here are some important exercises that can develop strength in these movements. Keep in mind that these exercises represent only a few of many options.

Total-body Lifting

Your legs, hips and back are the workhorses when you lift a person off the mat in a match, so these are your primary areas to strengthen in the weight room.

The best total-body lifts to use include the power clean, deadlifts, and front squats or lunges. I would put them in that order in terms of their specificity to wrestling. Depending on the time of the year, you might use some lifts more than others based on your goals. Later you will read about how to use specific lifts at various times of the year.

Power cleans involve starting in a position that is similar to a wrestling stance and finishing with the weight held up by your chest area, just like lifting an opponent.

The key is to perform power cleans fast and explosively. This develops your speed-strength called power. Deadlifts begin in the same position as a power clean (right), but the emphasis on this move is to develop slow-speed strength,

rather than power. Therefore, this exercise might be more of an off-season exercise.

Front squats or overhead squats should be key lifts in your strength program because they force you to keep an erect torso, and, with front squats, the weight is held in front of you more in the position you would hold an opponent.

FRONT SQUAT : In a front squat the weight is in front of you like when you lift an opponent.

OVERHEAD SQUAT POSITION: Holding a barbell overhead strengthens torso musculature and provides an excellent total-body strength benefit.

You can get a great workout using less weight than you can with back squats, because it is harder to do them. You can do front squats without a barbell, such as using heavy bags, a training partner or even holding a weight out at arms' length, which strengthens your abdominals and lower back.

If you are looking for even more movement specificity, lunges may be the best leg exercise you can do. You are in a lunged position when you hit a stand-up, penetrate on a leg attack or just putting on your ankle strap before the match! Lunges are not considered total body exercises, but you can increase the number of muscles dynamically activated by doing a twisting lunge with a weight plate or a medicine ball (below) or by simply holding a dumbbell in one hand to force you keep your balance.

TWISTING LUNGE START POSITION: Modify traditional lifts to make them wrestling-specific.

TWISTING LUNGE MIDPOINT: Twist to both sides while performing walking lunges.

Whether you do walking lunges or just step forward and backward is a matter of preference. Walking lunges simulate penetrating on a takedown attempt; whereas stepping forward and backward approximates pushing back into an opponent like you do when you hit a stand-up.

Rotational Movements

Most sports involve some type of rotational movement, but in wrestling you rotate and twist against your opponent's resistance so rotational strength is very important. Muscles in your torso (also called "core" musculature) including erector spinae, rectus abdominals, and internal and external obliques all contribute to the effort. You can develop your rotational strength in many ways, but my favorite exercises involve a stability ball and a dumbbell or weight plate. The ball will roll slightly as you do a variety of exercises. As you attempt to maintain balance you will call upon numerous muscles to help stabilize yourself.

Prone rocking is perfect for challenging the muscles needed to defend the gut wrench in freestyle and Greco-Roman wrestling.

GUT WRENCH: Prone rocking helps you defense against the gut wrench.

PRONE ROCKING: Try to touch elbows on floor on both sides.

Rock side to side as far as possible but without letting your feet come off the floor. As you improve, challenge yourself by putting your feet closer together. Supine rotations (below) allow you to twist a little further and engage the adductor muscles of you inner thighs as well.

DUMBBELL SUPINE ROTATIONS: Twist your torso while you rotate the weight to both sides.

You can easily engage your core musculature by modifying traditional exercises and using an exercise ball, such as doing single-arm bench presses or flies. Chapter five describes several exercises made more functional with the exercise ball.

SINGLE-ARM DUMBBELL FLY: Single-arm exercises performed on a ball engage all the stabilizing muscles.

Pulling and Squeezing

Any exercise that simulates squeezing an opponent is important for you. To strengthen these muscles, perform a variety of pulling movements, specifically rowing exercises. I prefer rowing exercises where my hands are close together, because that is most similar to bear hugging an opponent. This exercise can also be modified and performed standing, which involves more core musculature.

ROWING EXERCISE FROM WRESTLING STANDING POSITION: Pull the cables or bands towards your chest.

Doing pull-up knee lifts as shown in the right photo below strengthens your pulling muscles and develops core musculature in ways that will help you build good base during bottom-position mat wrestling.

Good bottom-position wrestling is compact with knees and elbows close together.

PULL-UP KNEE RAISES: Perform a reverse-grip pull-up and draw your knees to your elbows at the top position.

Begin the exercise with a reverse grip or a parallel grip. As you pull yourself up begin raising your knees and tucking your body into a ball until the end of the movement when your knees or inner thighs should be touching your elbows.

You can modify nearly any traditional weight room exercise to be more challenging when you use your imagination. If you find yourself without equipment, be creative and find a similar alternative. For example, rope climbing is an excellent exercise for wrestlers, but if you don't have access to a rope, you can do towel saws as shown below to develop your upper-body strength.

TOWEL SAW: Hang from the towel and alternately pull on the ends of the towel like you were using it to saw through something. Very tough!

Intensity Specificity

Which is more important for wrestling, being *strong* or *powerful*? Do you know the difference? Strength is an ability to apply force, but power adds the dimension of speed to the movement. You need both in wrestling.

Static and Dynamic Strength

Strength can be static or dynamic. Static strength, sometimes called isometric strength, occurs when a muscle is tense but there is no change in the length of the muscle. This morning when you flexed your biceps in the mirror you were isometrically contracting your muscle. Dynamic strength means that the muscle is lengthening or shortening under tension. When you perform an arm curl, you are developing dynamic strength.

Both static and dynamic strength are critical in wrestling. Every time you hold a person in a move you use your static strength. Most of the time you use static and dynamic strength simultaneously, such as holding a person in a control tie with your arms (static), and dynamically contracting your leg and trunk muscles to position your body for a leg attack.

The best way to develop static strength is with isometric exercise, which you could perform by squeezing something. Unfortunately, isometrics only increase your strength in the position you are performing the exercise. Thus, the best way to increase your isometric strength for wrestling is by wrestling. Hundreds of reps of putting a training partner or an opponent in a front headlock, for example, will isometrically strengthen everything necessary.

Dynamic strength is the basis for all weight room exercises. You can have strength at a wide range of speeds. You may have noticed that you can move lighter weights faster than you can move heavy weights. This raises the question of how fast you should lift a weight to best prepare you to wrestle. After all, most movements in wrestling are much faster than

Sprint-holds

Have you ever had a tough opponent on his or her back in a match and used so much energy that you wondered whether you would have the energy to keep wrestling if you didn't get the pin? I was never more worried than when I had a tough opponent on his back. My solution when I became a coach was to have my wrestlers do "sprint-holds." Sprint-holds involve two partners. The first one runs a sprint, usually back and forth across the wrestling room, while the second one holds himself on a pull-up bar or a rope. The person on the pull-up bar hangs with arms flexed and knees drawn up as far as possible in a fetal position (page 69). This is the isometric part of the exercise. I felt that this would build a wrestler's confidence in being able to use a lot of energy isometrically and then be able to continue hammering if the dude got off his back.

you can move the weight of your one-repetition max.

Slow-speed and High-speed Exercise

When you see a wrestler that is explosive, you notice how fast and powerful he or she executes moves. If given the choice, most wrestlers would probably want to be fast and explosive rather than just being strong. However, a lot of people think that this means it is more important to lift a lighter weight fast than to lift a heavier weight, which you can only do slowly.

The fact is that slow-speed movements in the weight room increase your overall strength and enable you to move all weights faster. For example, if your max on the bench press was 150 pounds, you probably would not move that amount of weight very fast on that lift. However, if your increased your strength to 250 pounds, you would be able to move 150 pounds a lot faster and more explosively.

If you had to choose between doing a light weight fast and a heavy weight as fast as you can (which would still be slow), pick the heavier weight. A light weight limits the amount of force you need to use, because you coast through much of the lifting phase, so you can control the weight. Imagine doing a bench press with about 30% of your one-repetition max (1-RM). If you push the bar as fast as possible off your chest, you are strong enough to create such momentum in the first couple of inches that you would literally throw it off your chest if you applied a full effort through the full press. On the other hand, if you are training with 80% or 90% of your 1-RM, the weight is heavy enough that you have to push as hard as possible through the entire range of motion.

This isn't to say that you should never train with high speed in the weight room. Just use equipment that can safely be thrown, such as a bag of sand or a medicine ball. (In case you were wondering, a "medicine ball" is a soft, weighted ball, often the size of a basketball.) When your intent is to throw something, you don't need to slow it down, so you can go as hard as possible through the entire range of motion. Throwing a medicine ball (right) is an excellent way to train with high-speed in a chest-pressing movement. You can develop high-speed strength with a squat exercise by hugging a weight to your chest and doing jump squats.

MEDICINE BALL BENCH PRESS THROWS: Throwing objects allows you to apply full force through a full range of joint motion.

Of the traditional weight room lifts, power cleans, snatches and overhead pushing exercises work best for high-speed lifting, although you still need a fairly high percentage of your 1-RM, so that momentum does not become an issue. Using about 75-85% of your one-rep max for these exercises will develop your strength, but allow you to move the weight quickly. You can also use dumbbells for most power exercises.

Body weight exercises (called plyometrics) are becoming increasingly popular for developing power. These exercises make use of the energy that your muscles and tendons create when you rapidly stretch them. You can picture how this works by imagining yourself doing a vertical jump. When you do a vertical jump, you squat rapidly and then explode upward. The rapid squat puts a stretch on your muscles similar to stretching a thick rubber band and gives you more power. Muscle spindles, protective structures in muscle tissue, do a lot of the work by causing intense contractions that increase your jump height.

Probably the best lower-body plyometrics exercise for wrestlers is a cycled split squat jump (we might call them "penetration jumps"), because it is similar to the leg position on many penetration steps for leg attacks.

PENETRATION JUMPS: Explosively lunge upwards and switch legs in the air. Allow your back knee to nearly touch the floor when landing.

You can also perform lateral bounding as shown at left. Lateral bounding is an excellent way to develop the explosiveness required for a high crotch leg attack.

LATERAL BOUNDING: Visualize yourself driving at an angle against an opponent like when you are driving across an opponent on a leg attack.

Clapping push-ups is a good upper-body exercise. The nature of wrestling practice provides numerous opportunities to do exercises that are similar in nature to plyometrics; therefore, you probably don't need to dedicate a lot of time to them. One or two exercises included as part of your strength workout is probably sufficient. An internet search will provide you with pictures and videos of many different options. Choose the ones that you think are the most specific to wrestling.

Treat plyometrics like any weight room exercise. Give yourself plenty of rest between sets. A work-to-rest ratio of about 1:5 would be about right. Therefore, if it takes you 20 seconds to do a set of eight or 10 jumps, then you would rest about 90 seconds to two minutes between sets. Focus on the quality of your movement rather than rushing to complete them even if you don't feel tired. If you perform plyometrics in the same workout as a heavy lifting session or wrestling practice, do them early in the workout while you are still fresh, so you are as explosive as possible.

Choosing the Right Exercises

Each time you workout you will be faced with deciding which exercises to include. It's not necessary to perform all possible exercises for a movement in every workout. One or two exercises will be sufficient. You can rotate your exercises so you are doing something slightly different in each workout or use one exercise for a few weeks and then switch to another. Just make sure that each workout includes total body lifts, rotational movements, and pulling and squeezing. I have focused on exercises that would be most specific to wrestling, but that does not mean you should not incorporate other exercises into your program. Any exercises can be added to your program to increase your overall strength.

Here are two examples of workouts that develop overall strength and wrestling-specific strength. The numbers of sets and reps would be appropriate for a wrestler that has been doing this type of training for several weeks.

Overall- and Wrestling-Specific Strength Workouts	
In-season workout	Off-season workout
General warm-up (jogging) 10 min.	General warm-up (stationary bike) 10 min.
Specific warm-up (joint rotational exercises)	Specific warm-up (cartwheels & tumbling)
Power clean from floor 3 sets of 5 (3x5)	Deadlift (5x8)
Walking lunge with a twist (3x6 each leg)	Back squat (5x8)
Reverse grip bent-over row (3x8)	Incline dumbbell bench press (5x8)
Single-arm dumbbell bench press on ball (3x8)	Hamstring/leg curls (3x12 each leg)
Prone rocking (3x 6 each way)	Neck bridges w/hands support (30 sec.)
Cool down (stationary bike)	Rope climb (3 x 25-foot rope) OR
	Towel pull-ups (3 x 10-12)
	Cool down and stretching

You probably noticed the differences between the two workouts. The in-season workout included fewer exercises, sets, and reps than the off-season workout, because there is a greater demand on your body during wrestling season. The fact that I used jogging in one warm-up and biking in the other of these workouts doesn't really matter. However, in the off-season workout, I incorporated gymnastics movements, because you probably won't be doing them if you are not having daily wrestling practice.

Power cleans are a good in-season total-body exercise, because they focus on speed, whereas deadlifts, a slow-speed exercise, emphasize strength, so I put those in the off-season. Likewise a walking lunge is more specific to wrestling movement than the back squat, so that is included in the in-season workout. Using dumbbells for the incline bench press and doing leg curls one leg at a time, reinforce the fact that arms and legs work independently in a wrestling. I added neck bridges and stretching to the off-season workout, because you will not have those programmed into your daily workout if you are not in wrestling practice.

This strategy gives you an overview of a philosophy of strength training for in-season and off-season workouts. When you develop your own programs, incorporate the wrestling-specific movements and train both traditional and specific exercises.

Functional resistance training "farmer strength"

Recently, strength and conditioning gurus have focused heavily on exercises to duplicate natural body movements to the furthest extent possible. Instead of being limited to deadlifts, for example, strength coaches are having their athletes flipping tractor tires. Rather than spending hundreds of dollars on machines designed to work the abdominals, Crossfit® gyms are purchasing sledge hammers and having their members beat on tires. All the collective knowledge we have gained about strength training has brought us back to what Milo, the legendary wrestler of Croton, knew thousands of years ago. (It is said that he developed his legendary strength by carrying a newborn ox every day until it was full grown.) Perhaps the best way to develop wrestling strength is to get a job on a farm or a construction crew and then to work hard!

Stability-limited Exercises

HOW STRONG IS STRONG ENOUGH?

If you wanted to play college or pro football, you could find information about how strong and fast you would need to be for a coach to even *consider* you as a recruit. In many cases, how a high school or college football player performs in combines (events that measure strength and speed) is a critical factor in whether he makes it to the next level. Wrestling coaches don't factor in strength or speed when they evaluate a prospect—unless someone is obviously very weak.

Nevertheless, strength is important for wrestling success. But how strong must you be for wrestling, and how do you know when you have achieved enough strength? Unfortunately, there are no magical formulas to tell you that answer. Someone can test your 1-RM in the weight room to see how much you can bench press, but lifting with a balanced weight where your body is fully supported is not very wrestling specific. Limiting your training to the traditional exercises you see people doing in the weight room will not fully develop the functional strength you need in wrestling. Much of your training should involve stability-limited exercises, which are exercises you perform when you are struggling to maintain balance.

People do most of the traditional ("core") weight room exercises like the power clean, squat, and bench press each week. This training frequency lends itself well to the planned progressions you will read about in chapter six. However, there are literally hundreds of stability-limited exercises and it is more important to challenge yourself with a variety of these movements than to develop a progression towards achieving a strong one-repetition maximum with a few of these types of exercises. That is why the workouts in the appendix only include progression schemes for core lifts and will require you to select from the stability-limited exercises in this chapter.

Most of the exercises in this chapter are similar to traditional lifts, but they have been modified to reduce stability (in the case of those performed on the stability ball) or to decrease the balance of the load, such as single-dumbbell exercises. The best thing about these exercises is that each of them can be done with the limited equipment shown at left.

GOOD, BETTER, BEST!

Balance requires active musculature, so the more off-balance you are when doing any exercise the more muscles you activate and the better it is for wrestling. Exercises performed on a stability ball get tougher when you narrow your base of support or when you support your body weight over a greater distance.

Stability Ball Push-up Lockout Position

GOOD: Two hands on ball provides a wide base of support.

BETTER: Narrowing the base of support under your shoulders will require more activation of your core musculature.

BEST!: Try a one-handed push-up from this position.

SINGLE-FIST PUSH-UP LOCKOUT POSITION: Try this with your feet close together for an even greater challenge!

More Stability Ball Progressions

GOOD: SHINS ON BALL.
This provides the most surface area and stability for support. Don't allow your hips to sag.

BETTER: TOES ON BALL.
Here all the stabilization is provided by the hip flexors and muscles of the trunk.

BEST!: ONE FOOT ON BALL.
Achieve your balance with both feet on the ball and then raise one foot. Repeat for both legs.

GOOD: TWO-BALL BENT ARM FLY.
This not only strengthens your chest and shoulders, it engages hip flexors and abdominals.

More Stability Ball Progressions

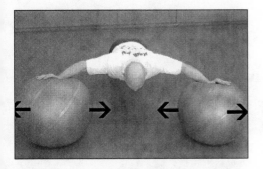

BETTER: TWO-BALL CROSS ROLLOUTS.
You can roll the balls directly to the side or at a 45˚ angle from the line of your spine.

GOOD: PRONE PIKE.
Start this exercise in a push-up position with your feet on the ball. Draw the ball towards you as you flex your hips to elevate your butt.

BETTER: BALL ROLLOUT PLANK.
"Best" would be to do this with one arm. If you can do it, send me a picture!

BALANCE PROGRESSIONS FOR THE EXERCISE BALL

Begin by balancing on your hands and knees and then work to kneeling on the ball, and, finally, standing on the ball.

BALL BALANCE STAGE I: Start with your knees on the ball and your hands on the floor. Gradually shift your weight towards your hips and legs as your bring one hand and then the other to the ball.

BALL BALANCE STAGE II: Begin dumbbell lifting from this position. When you are learning this, it will be easier if you flex your hips slightly.

BALL BALANCE STAGE III: Paying attention to where your feet are on the ball will make it easier to get on without using your hands.

After you have mastered standing on the ball, begin doing traditional lifting exercises. You may want to begin with two dumbbells to help you maintain balance, then progress to one dumbbell.

LIFTING ON BALL STAGE I: With this exercise you can quickly work up to whatever load you lift while standing on the floor.

LIFTING ON BALL STAGE II: An intermediate progression would be to use two dumbbells for better balance.

LIFTING ON BALL STAGE III: Squats on the ball are more challenging when you hold a weight directly over your head.

STABILITY BALL EXERCISES

No exercise performed on the stability ball isolates a body part or a muscle group, but listing them as such makes it easier to pick the ones that will fit well with any core exercises you may be doing in the same workout. These are by no means the limit to what you can do with an exercise ball. Use your imagination!

Balancing Exercises

Each of these exercises is designed to increase your body awareness and balance. When weights are used, such as in the ball balance curl press and the ball balance trunk twists, the goal is to enhance the demands on your balance more than developing absolute strength for that movement.

BALL BALANCE SUPERMAN: This is a timed exercise work up to 30 seconds, then add arm and leg fluttering movements to increase the demand on your core musculature.

Ball Balance Curl-press

START: As you progress from ball balance stage I to stage III, it is easier if you hold the weight against the ball as you use your free hand to stabilize the ball.

MIDPOINT: As you curl the weight, you will need to adjust your center of gravity to maintain your balance, so go slowly at first.

FINISH: It's easiest to keep your balance if you focus your gaze on a spot on the floor about 10 feet in front of you.

Ball Balance Trunk Twist

Rotate side to side keeping your knees flexed about 45°. Avoid rotating quickly. This is not a power exercise.

Use the ball balance wrestling stance (below) to prepare for more complex movements from that position such as arm curls, shoulder presses, and overhead squats (bottom).

Ball Balance Wrestling Stance

Adding single-arm dumbbell exercises, such as shoulder presses or lateral raises develops core strength.

Ball Balance Overhead Squat

START   BOTTOM POSITION

Squatting is more difficult than other weighted exercises performed on a ball. Begin without weight with your arms extended from your body for balance. Progress to holding your hands in a prayer position over your head, and, finally to holding a weight as shown

Prone Pike

When returning from the pike position to the starting position, be sure to push the ball away from your body. Push back until your hands are under your shoulders or slightly in front of them rather than under your chest.

Prone Pike Single-leg Variation

Keep the elevated leg as straight and as high as your flexibility allows. Make sure to switch legs. This position is also an excellent variation for push-ups.

Prone Trunk Rotations

START

FINISH

Start in a push-up position with your toes on the ball. Flex your hips and knees to about 90°.

Roll the ball side to side each direction. The trunk rotation occurs as much from lowering your hip towards the floor as from rolling the ball to the side.

Prone Hyperextension

From this position, lower your trunk until your hands touch the floor, and then return to the starting position.

Leg Exercises

The versatility of the stability ball makes it easy to duplicate wrestling positions with leg exercises. Adding weight makes these movements even more difficult.

SINGLE-LEG LATERAL WALL SQUAT: Perform single-leg squats by alternately flexing and extending the knee with the other leg lifted off the floor. This may also be done by driving off the inside leg and elevating the outside leg.

HIGH CROTCH POSITION: Notice the similar body position of the driving position of this high crotch and the single-leg lateral wall squat.

SINGLE-LEG, BACK-PRESSURE WALL SQUAT: You may need to begin by working off two legs.

STAND-UP: Effective stand-ups require a certain amount of back pressure.

Ball Bridge Supine Knee Flexion-Extension

Strengthen your hamstrings by flexing and extending your knees as if you were doing a reverse knee curl. Keep the line between your shoulders and knees straight by lifting your hips as you flex your knees.

If you need more stability, put your hands on the floor out to sides of your hips. Make it tougher by crossing your arms over your chest.

Chest, Shoulder, and Upper Back Exercises

These exercises are unmatched for developing the upper-body strength in the way you use it in a wrestling match. You can increase the difficulty level by using balls of different sizes for exercises requiring two stability balls.

Variations of a Traditional Push-up

BALL PUSH-UP LOCKOUT (START): Begin your push-ups from this position. Putting your feet together will increase the difficulty.

PUSH-UP POSITION ON FISTS ON TWO BALLS:
This can be made easier by keeping your hands flat on the balls or more difficult by lifting one foot off the floor. Also try adding a third ball and to place your feet upon!

TWO-BALL EXTENSION ROLLOUTS:
Begin in the two-ball push-up position. Roll each ball away from you and towards you in an alternating pattern. As one ball rolls out, the other is coming in.

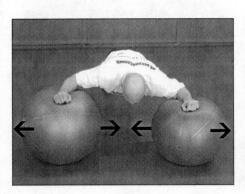

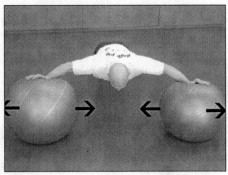

TWO-BALL BENT-ARM FLY: Begin in with your elbows under your chest. Adduct your arms out to the side keeping your elbows bent.

TWO-BALL STRAIGHT-ARM FLY: Begin in the two-ball push-up position. Adduct your arms so the ball rolls away from you. Increase the challenge by lifting one foot!

Explosive lockouts begin in a push-up position with your hands on a ball. Remove your hands from the ball and extend your arms out the side as if you are flying. Allow your chest to bounce off the ball, and then catch yourself back on the ball in push-up position. You can make this exercise tougher by landing on the ball with one hand or on your fist. When you get good at it, you can do several reps alternating which hand you land on.

EXPLOSIVE LOCKOUTS (MIDFLIGHT!): Spot where you will place your hands as you bounce off the ball.

EXPLOSIVE LOCKOUTS (SINGLE-ARM FINISH): Avoid trying to plant your hand on the ball too early after bouncing off your chest. Allowing enough clearance will enable you to plant with a straighter and stronger arm.

DUMBBELL ROW WITH FIST ON BALL: The more weight you put on your fist, the harder this exercise becomes. For the ultimate stability challenge try lifting your back leg!"

BALL BALANCE SINGLE-ARM LATERAL RAISE: Begin with the dumbbell held at your side. Raise it out to the side about shoulder level.

BALL BALANCE SINGLE-ARM FRONT RAISE: You can turn this into a tougher combination exercise be raising the dumbbell all the way over your head and then descending into a single arm overhead squat

STANDING ON BALL DUMBBELLS IN HANDS: When working to stand on the ball with a dumbbell in each hand press the dumbbells against the ball to stabilize. Shift your hips further backward to counterbalance the dumbbells.

MAKING TRADITIONAL EXERCISES MORE FUNCTIONAL

Unbalancing traditional weight room exercises is as simple as using a single dumbbell when performing the lift. Some examples were shown in chapter four. When you first train in this manner, you will probably use a lot lighter weight than when you perform the same exercises with a barbell or two dumbbells, but you will quickly progress to more weight. And when this happens, you will be strong…very strong.

Single-Arm Dumbbell Lifts

ONE-ARM DUMBBELL CLEAN AND PRESS (START): Straddle the dumbbell and keep it close to your body as you pull it from the floor and past your hips and belly button.

(FINISH): If you progress to using a heavier weights, you will not be able to press the weight over your head with just your arm strength. You must drive it up with your legs. This adds to the functionality of the lift.

Turkish get-ups (below) strengthen your shoulder while engaging all your core musculature. Begin light and progress to a weight you can only do once or twice. Emphasize strength and movement quality rather than doing a lot of reps. If you do attempt more than one rep, lower the weight and start over. Don't try to sit back down while holding a heavy weight over your head.

Turkish Get-ups

START: The key to progressing from Step II to Step III is to keep the dumbbell directly over your shoulder.

STEP II: Your first movement will be to rotate your body to the side that is not holding the weight.

STEP III: From here, continue to rise until you are standing on both feet with the dumbbell over head.

INJURY-PREVENTING EXERCISES WRESTLERS NEVER DO

If someone were to ask me to tell them the most commonly injured body part for wrestlers, I'd have to say the shoulders and knees…and backs…and probably necks. I guess that kind of means it's easier to list the areas that aren't prone to injury. Sometimes these injuries are "acute," which means they happen all at once. Other times they are "chronic;" they just kind of happen over time. In either case, a little preventative exercise can go a long way to keeping you healthy. Here are a few good ones that you should do for a couple sets of 10-20 reps every few workouts.

Lunging windmills (below) stretch out your hips, help with your balance and strengthen the muscles of your lower back. To do these, get into a deep lunge so that your front knee is bent to about 90°. Lean your torso forward until your chest nearly touches your front thigh. Extend your arms as if you are flying and rotate your upper body so that you are alternately touching your front foot with each hand.

LUNGING WINDMILLS: Try to keep a straight line between the ankle of your back leg through your spine to the top of your head. Turn the back foot out to 45° if necessary.

Another great exercise for the lower back is a prone snow angel (below). This will strengthen the muscles of your butt and back without the use of weights. Vary this exercise by putting your arms over head and your feet close together and then fluttering both arms and legs up and down.

PRONE SNOW ANGELS: Perform these like you were doing jumping jacks while lying on your belly. Keep your toes 3-4 inches off the floor, which will be more difficult as you spread your feet wide.

You know that area in your lower back that gets sore after the first few days of practice? Right above your butt cheeks on either side of your spine? Yeah, that's the area! Doing reverse woodchoppers (below), barbell lateral trunk flexion (page 97) and supine leg swings (page 97) will get that area in shape before the season begins.

REVERSE WOODCHOPPERS: Keep your back straight when doing this. At the upper and lower positions you can twist your trunk slightly in the direction of the reach. This also works well with elastic bands.

LATERAL TRUNK FLEXION: This is an advanced exercise. Beginners should sit on a ball and do the movement with no weight.

SUPINE LEG SWINGS: Swing your feet side to side. Keep your upper back flat on the floor and your hips flexed as close to 90° as possible. An easier modification is to do this with bent knees.

Low-bridge shoulder touches (below) go one step beyond the high bridges (on the top of your head) that most wrestlers usually do in practices. When someone is trying to pin you (Heaven forbid!), you will probably not be in the high bridge position. You need to strengthen your neck to be strong when your shoulders are mere inches off the mat. Low bridges are tough because you're using more of your muscles to hold you up rather than posting on top of your head, so they will develop great neck strength. Get into a low bridge and then alternate touching each shoulder on the mat.

LOW-BRIDGE SHOULDER TOUCHES: Bridge on the back of your head rather than on the top of your head. Keep your hips low and alternate touching each shoulder on the mat.

Finally, you must not neglect the rotator cuff muscles of shoulders. The shoulder is a ball-and-socket joint, so it can move in many directions. Traditional weight room exercises usually only strengthen the muscles of the shoulder for a few movements, which creates strength imbalances that can increase injury risk. Do one or two sets of 10-20 reps for each of the following exercises as a warm-up before every strength training workout. Your shoulders will thank you for it. Jumping rope is also a good exercise for your shoulders, because it provides dozens of reps in a position similar to the shoulder external rotation. Another thing you can do to keep your shoulders happy is to stay off the bottom in your matches and avoid getting stuck underneath a guy who sprawls when you shoot! Ahhh, if it were only that easy...

Reverse Fly Scapula Retraction

Pinch your shoulder blades together as you raise your thumbs towards the ceiling. Do this in three arm positions: straight out from your body (90˚), slightly above (135˚) and a little below (45˚).

Shoulder External Rotation

START (LEFT): The objective is to rotate your arm away from your body while stabilizing your scapula (shoulder blade). Some people pinch a rolled up towel under their arm while doing this exercise

FINISH (RIGHT): Squeeze your elbow toward your ribs and your shoulder blades toward your spine as you do this exercise.

Shoulder Internal Rotation

Internal rotations tend to be easier than external rotations. You can increase the resistance by stretching the elastic band further or adding weight if you are using a cabled weight machine.

START   FINISH

Abducted External Rotation

When performing this exercise, it is more important that you go through your full range of motion than using great resistance. You can achieve greater rotation if you press your scapula down and towards your spine to engage the muscles.

Abducted Internal Rotation

Although not shown here, you can achieve a greater range of motion in the finish position (without pulling the band across your shoulder) if you anchor your band higher on the wall so it is above your shoulder. You can also do this exercise from your knees.

MATCH-A-DAY WORKOUTS

A few years ago I read an article in <u>Runner's World</u> magazine about people called "streakers." It's not what you're thinking. These are folks who have maintained long streaks of never missing a day of running. Some of these streaks have lasted 30 years or more! They inspired me to start my own streak. About 20 months into my own streak of running at least a mile a day, I came up with the idea of the match-a-day workout. Running is good for your cardiovascular system, but it doesn't do much for strengthening your back, neck or arms the way that you use them in wrestling. I thought about how wrestlers could benefit, if they pushed themselves at wrestling-match intensity for at least six or eight minutes every day. You might not have time to go to the gym for an hour, but six minutes of intense work every day adds up to over 36 hours of intense training each year—and that's assuming you wouldn't do anything else.

The following match-a-day workouts are designed to get your heart rate elevated and give you a total-body workout with a small amount of equipment when you have a limited amount of time. These workouts last between eight and 12 minutes depending on how many times you go through each rotation. Below are seven workouts (the first week of your "streak") to get you started. Use these workouts each week or develop your own match-a-day workouts. How long will you keep your streak alive?

Day 1

Equipment: Pull-up bar
Instructions: Perform each exercise for 45 seconds; rest 15 seconds between each exercise; repeat if desired.
Pull-up knee-lifts (page 69)
Penetration jumps (page 73)
Squat thrusts*

Spin drill (get in a tripod with your hands on the floor, shuffle your feet to spin each direction - see below)

Supine leg swings (page 97)

Low bridge shoulder touches (page 97)

Prone snow angels (page 96)

Clapper push-ups

*Begin standing with your arms extended upwards. Drop to a four-point stance (palms of hands and feet on floor), then drop to a full push-up. Jump back to the four-point stance, then return to the starting position. That's one rep.

SPIN DRILL: Move laterally as quickly as possible; alternate going each direction. It is not necessary to rotate in a full circle.

Day 2

Equipment: One dumbbell and one stability ball

Instructions: Perform each exercise for 45 seconds; rest 15 seconds between each exercise; repeat if desired.

Single-arm dumbbell clean and press (page 94)

Twisting lunge walk holding dumbbell to chest (page 66)

Prone rocking (page 67)

Stability ball push-up (page 90)

Dumbbell row on ball (page 92)

Ball balance supine knee flexion (page 90)

y 3

uipment: Two dumbbells, pull-up bar, and two stability balls

structions: Do each exercise for 30 seconds; rest 15 seconds between

ch; repeat the workout two times.

mbbell clean and press (page 94)

teral bounding (page 74)

nt-arm hanging jackknives (below)

verse wood choppers holding the ends of one dumbbell (page 96)

vo ball straight-arm fly (page 91)

ternating dumbbell upright row (below)

BENT-ARM HANGING JACKKNIVES: Keep legs as straight as possible. Avoid swinging. This may also be done with straight arms. Once you reach the top position, you can also "windshield wiper" your legs side to side.

ALTERNATING DUMBBELL UPRIGHT ROW: Pull each dumbbell from the low position to the high position. Use a weight that will pose a challenge but not so heavy that you would need to throw your body into the effort.

Day 4

Equipment: One stability ball

Instructions: Perform each exercise for one minute; rest 15 seconds between exercises; repeat two times.

Single-leg lateral wall squats (page 89)

Single-leg prone pike (page 87)

Ball Bridge Supine Knee Flexion-Extension (page 90)

Explosive Lockouts (page 92)

Ball back extension (page 88)

Day 5

Equipment: Two dumbbells (weight you can curl no more than 10 times)

Instructions: Perform each exercise for one minute; rest 15 seconds between exercises; repeat two times.

Dumbbell clean and press (page 94)

Dumbbell clock lunge and reach (below left)

Dumbbell upright row (page 103, raising both dumbbells simultaneously)

Dumbbell pummel uppercut (right)

Low-bridge shoulder touches (page 97)

DUMBBELL CLOCK LUNGE AND REACH: Lunge several directions of the clock face: Noon, 6 o'clock, 3 o'clock etc. Reach the dumbbells to the floor in each position as shown.

DUMBBELL PUMMEL UPPERCUT: Alternate raising each dumbbell in front of you. Imagine digging for an underhook or throwing an uppercut in boxing.

Day 6

Equipment: Pull-up bar and stability ball

Instructions: Perform each exercise for 30 seconds; no rest between exercises; repeat three times.

Squat-thrust pull-ups*   Ball balance squats (page 86)

Prone trunk rotations (page 88)   Towel saw (page 69)

Ball rollout plank (page 81)

*Begin standing under a pull-up bar that requires you to jump to reach it. Drop to a four-point stance (palms and feet on floor), then drop to a full push-up. Jump back to the four-point stance then leap up to the bar and complete a pull-up.

Day 7

Equipment: Barbell and weights, pull-up bar

Instructions: Perform each exercise for 1 minute; repeat three times separated by 30 seconds.

Front Squat (page 65)   Climber crunches (below)

Reverse-grip barbell row (below)   Penetration jumps (page 73)

CLIMBER CRUNCHES START: Slowly draw a knee to the opposite elbow while hanging from the bar.

CLIMBER CRUNCHES FINISH: Alternate legs with each rep and avoid swinging.

REVERSE-GRIP BARBELL ROW: Maintain a flat lower back position throughout the movement.

CHAPTER 6
Developing Your Annual Lifting Plan
Year-round Athlete

PROGRESSION

Have you ever trained for several weeks and then felt "stale" for no apparent reason? If so, it is possible that you may have been overtrained. Overtraining occurs when you work hard, but do not vary the intensity and volume of your workouts. Many people think that overtraining only happens with endurance exercise, but it can happen in strength training also. In chapter four I mentioned that hormones are responsible for increasing your muscle size. Some hormones actually break down muscle tissue in response to starvation and overtraining. If you try to maintain a high volume of strength training when you are having hard wrestling practices, you run the risk of overtraining and having an undesired hormonal response.

Progression involves planned variations in how many days per week you train, how long your workouts last and how hard they are. An effective progression scheme will help you to peak at the right time though manipulating the intensity and volume of your workouts and varying the type of exercises you do to make them more wrestling-specific as you get closer to competition.

Training Frequency

Generally, strength training programs are three days per week and incorporate a day of recovery in between each training day. The rule-of-thumb is to give the muscles you've trained at least 48 hours to recover before doing a similar exercise. Some workouts are four or six days per week. These split routines are common in off-season training and among bodybuilders who perform several exercises per body part in each workout. The table below shows two common training frequencies used by people who have been influenced by the programs of bodybuilders.

Four- and Six-Day Split Strength Training Weeks			
Four Training Days		Six Training Days	
Mon.	Chest, Shoulders,Triceps	Mon.	Chest, Shoulders,Triceps
Tues.	Back, Legs, Biceps	Tues.	Back, Biceps
Wed.	OFF	Wed.	Legs
Thurs.	Chest, Shoulders,Triceps	Thurs.	Chest, Shoulders,Triceps
Fri.	Back, Legs, Biceps	Fri.	Back, Biceps
Sat.	OFF	Sat.	Legs
Sun.	OFF	Sun.	OFF

You may notice that the emphasis in these split routines is on training a body *part* not a body *movement* or an exercise. That is the difference between a cosmetic approach to lifting and a performance approach like you need for wrestling. Unless you have a need to increase muscle size significantly, such as needing to get big enough to wrestle at a higher weight class, you shouldn't need to lift more than two or three times per week.

With strength training, less is more. Here comes a no-brainer: the harder your workouts, the longer it takes you to recover from them. Profound, right? The problem is that wrestlers may know this, but their workouts don't reflect it. Usually wrestlers try to work out as hard as possible every training day, but don't vary the intensity or volume over time. When you consider how hard you've been training, it is important to think about the total stress load on your body, which includes any physical work. It's easy to see that if you have two-hour wrestling practices every day that you might have to cut back on the amount of strength training you do. But don't forget to take into consideration other factors like cutting weight or how a job that requires physical labor might influence your strength workouts.

Although three strength workouts per week is common in the off-season, the added training stress of in-season wrestling means that many wrestlers are better off with two workouts or even one workout during the season. My junior year in college was probably my best in terms of performance. I trained four days per week outside of the wrestling practice. Two days involved a 30-minute conditioning session using workouts similar to those in chapter 2 and two days were about 40 minutes of strength training. On the strength days I only did four lifts: deadlift, squat, bent-over-row, and bench press, each with 4-5 sets of 8 repetitions. Based on things I have learned since then, I would now include more power exercises, but the point is that I was able to maintain strength with only a few exercises. That was an optimal training program for me at that time in my athletic career, but everyone is different. You will have to experiment a little.

You will know when you have found the right frequency when your workouts challenge you, but you are fully recovered before the next strength session. If you plan to train one day, but you are still sore or a little tired from the previous workout, it's best to take the day off rather than push through. Recovery is the time when your body actually increases in strength, not during the workout. If you continue to beat your body and not allow for recovery, your training does little more than make you tired. When you are chronically tired, your body releases stress hormones that have a negative effect on your long-term improvement.

Hard Days and Easy Days

As mentioned in chapter one, overload involves pushing your body to do things at the limit of your ability. During traditional weight training exercises, in which you know exactly how much you are lifting, overload is measured relative to a maximum. Usually, this is a one-repetition max (1-RM), which is the amount you can lift no more than one time, but there are times when you might use a multiple-RM such as a 3-RM for your reference, such as if you are new to lifting weights or you are not very experienced with a particular exercise.

A measurable overload for a hard training workout would be 100% of what you can do. For example, a hard workout might be four sets of five reps (4x5) at 100% of your 5-RM. Medium and easy workouts, which still provide a training stimulus, are respectively 90% and 80% of the hard workout's load. Thus, an easy day might be 4 sets of 5 reps at 80% of your 5-RM.

	Overload Variation		
	Exercises	*Difficulty*	*Sets, Reps, Load*
Mon.	Front Squat, Incline Press, Row	Hard	5 x 8 x 8RM
Wed.	Front Squat, Incline Press, Row	Easy	5 x 8 @ 80% Mon. load
Fri.	Front Squat, Incline Press, Row	Medium	5 x 8 @ 90% Mon. load

You may wonder why wrestlers would even need to test a 1-RM. After all, your single-effort max is not as important in a match as having the endurance to wrestle for six or seven minutes. Testing your 1-RM will help you set loads and gauge your progress.

How to Test Your One-repetition Max

Many people spend too much time finding the exact amount they can lift during a "maxout" session. Ideally, you should be able to find your 1-RM within three to five maximum attempts. In fact, if you get somewhat close, within about 5-10% of your true max, you are close enough to establish accurate training intensities. To test your 1-RM, begin with a general warm-up followed by a few moderately heavy sets of about three to five reps. Your last warm-up set will probably be within 30-40 pounds of your first one-rep max attempt, depending on the exercise and your training status. If you fail at a 1-RM attempt, decrease the weight by half of what you put on the bar before that attempt. Rest two to four minutes between each 1-RM attempt, and always have a spotter!

Testing Your 1-RM		
General Warm-up	10 min. easy cardio	Achieve a light sweat
Warm-up set #1	5 reps	10-RM*
Warm-up set #2	4 reps	8-RM
Warm-up set #3	2-3 reps	5-RM
Begin one-rep max attempts†		
*Loads for warm-up sets are guesstimates of what you can do for prescribed reps. †Increase weight for each one-rep-max attempt about 10-20 pounds for upper body exercises and 20-30 pounds for leg or total body exercises.		

Sometimes people will *estimate* their 1-RM based on the number of reps they can do with a lighter weight. Charts are available to help with this, but they are not as accurate is the real thing. Use them only if testing a 1-RM is not possible.

Only test a 1-RM on the primary multi-joint exercises in your program such as power clean, squat, and bench press. There is little benefit to testing a 1-RM for single-joint (assistance) exercises such as biceps curls or leg curls. A 1-RM for single-joint exercises has no real application, and testing might increase your risk for an injury.

Sets, Reps, and Rest

The number of sets and reps you do determines the overall volume of your workout, and the amount of weight you lift is the intensity. Most athletic strength workouts range from three to five training sets, not including a few warm-up sets. Repetition ranges vary greatly, depending on the exercise, the stage of your training cycle and your goals.

Repetition-based or percentage-based loading?

You may have noticed that some workout programs assign the training load in terms of repetitions, such as 5 sets of 5, which implies you should use a weight you can only lift five times in a row. Other workouts prescribe training weight as a percentage of the 1-RM: 5 sets of 8 at 85% of 1-RM. Which is better? Usually it works best to assign a repetition-based load, because of the limitations of percentage-based load estimates. Percentage-based loads require you to know your one-rep max, which is not always practical. Another problem is that the number of repetitions people can perform with a given percentage of their 1-RM varies from person to person depending on their gender, training status, and the exercise they are doing. It is more common to see percentage-based programs in the Olympic lifts where the focus of each set is on quality of movement, not training to failure.

Reps per set based on the exercise and the goal

Power exercises should be performed with no more than five or six reps for weighted exercises like cleans, if the goal is strictly to develop power. If you want to develop power-endurance, it is best to use something like a weighted vest and duplicate the wrestling movement as much as possible. Thus, you might use power cleans to develop general power, but to develop power for driving into your opponent on a leg attack, use a weighted vest or a back pack and do 8-10 reps of that movement.

Slow-speed, multi-joint exercises, like the deadlift, squat and bench press, are called "core" exercises and will follow the repetition schemes in the periodized model on pages 112 and 113 For exercises that isolate a small area, like biceps and forearm curls, the number of reps should reflect how you use that muscle group in wrestling. Therefore, if you do these exercises, you should perform between 10 and 20 repetitions per set and keep the rest periods short.

Upper-end Repetitions per Set Based on Exercise Type		
	Reps	*Exercises**
Power	5-6	Power clean, Snatch, Pulling movements (e.g. clean pulls), Overhead pushes (push press, jerks etc.)
Power-Endurance	8-10	Jumps with weighted vest, Explosive wrestling movements with medicine ball.
Core	Varies†	Deadlift, Squat, Leg Press, Chest press and variations, Row variations, Shoulder Press
Assistance	10-20	Neck exercises, Elbow flexion and extension variations (curls etc.), ankle and knee exercises, forearm exercises.
Stability-Limited	Varies‡	Exercises performed on a stability ball
*Exercises for trunk are omitted; they are functionally trained with other exercises. †Repetitions for core exercises depend on the periodization stage. ‡Reps for a stability-limited exercise are the same for the exercise after which it was patterned.		

Here is an overview of how the number of sets and reps, and the between-set rest periods for core exercises should vary depending on your training goals.

Variations in Sets, Reps, and Rest Based on Training Goals			
Training Goal	Sets	Reps	Rest between sets
Hypertrophy (size increase)	3-6	6-12	30 sec. - 1.5 min.
Endurance	2-3	≥ 12	≤ 1 min.
General ("Basic") Strength	2-6	≤ 6	2 - 5 min.

Adapted with permission from T. R. Baechle, R. W. Earle, and D. Wathen, 2008, Resistance Training. In *Essentials of strength training and conditioning*, 3rd. Ed., edited by T. R. Baechle, R. W. Earle for the National Strength and Conditioning Association (Champaign, IL: Human Kinetics), 401, 406, 408.

A common mistake I see in the weight room is that people either rest too long when they are training for hypertrophy or they don't rest long enough when training for strength. It's difficult to maximize strength and endurance benefits in the weight room at the same time. Therefore, an annual training plan will help you focus on specific goals at different times of the year. In the off-season, for example, your goal might be to develop increased muscle size as you are growing. In the early and middle part of the season, you can focus on strength. By the end of the season, you will want to maintain your strength and maximize your wrestling performance. A periodized program will enable you to meet these training goals and peak at the right time.

PERIODIZATION

Most strength training requires that you push yourself to your limits in each workout. After several weeks, this takes a toll on your body. Accumulating fatigue can lead to staleness and overtraining. Many athletes understand the importance of frequently making changes to their workout routines and periodization is an extension of that philosophy. In a periodized program the number of sets, reps, and amount of recovery between sets vary throughout several months.

Periodized programs traditionally have the following phases.

Phases of a Periodized Program	
Phase	Purpose
Anatomical Adaptation	Prepare the body for lifting movements
Hypertrophy	Increase muscle size, prepare for heavier lifting
Basic Strength	Develop general strength to support a range of athletic activities
Power	Add the speed component to strength for sport-specific movements
Peaking	Maintain intensity but reduce volume and focus on competition

What happens in each phase depends on your needs. For example, if you have been doing power cleans for several months, you wouldn't need a period of anatomical adaptation for that lift. Likewise, as a wrestler your goals for peaking will be different than those of an athlete whose primary sport is the shot put. The length of time you stay in each phase depends on your needs and the time of the year.

The Periodized Program Adapted to Wrestling on page 115 is a periodized model adapted to the needs of wrestling, where peaking means that you have strength-endurance rather than a high one-rep max.

Notice how the volume of training (number of sets x number of reps) decreases as you progress from the hypertrophy through the basic strength phases and how the intensity (%1-RM) goes up. Decreasing the number of repetitions will reduce the risk of overtraining and the higher intensities at the end of this training cycle are most similar to the kind of force you need to use in competition.

Periodized Program Adapted to Wrestling					
Phase & Time of Year	# of weeks	Sets	Reps	% 1-RM	Rest
Anatomical Adaptation (any time needed)	2-3	2-3	12-15	50	1-2 min.
Hypertrophy (August-October)	8-12	3-6	8-12	50-75	30-90 sec.
Basic Strength (November-January)	6-12	3-5	4-8	80-95	2-5 min.
Strength-Endurance (Peaking) (February)	4	2-3	10-12	70-80	30 -60 sec.

If this was a program designed to increase your 1-RM, then the peaking phase would involve another increase in intensity and a decrease in repetitions. In this program your highest one-rep max would probably be somewhere in the middle of January. Because you can maintain a high percentage of your 1-RM for several weeks you will still have a high amount of maximum strength in February. However, your 1-RM is not as important in wrestling as having endurance to lift a high percentage of your maximum several times. Therefore, about a month prior to your state- or national-qualifying tournament increase your repetitions and decrease your rest periods. Be sure to decrease the number of sets are well. This will help you taper (reduce your training volume) and ensure you hit your peak at the right time.

You will probably find that you can do more repetitions at a given percentage of your 1-RM on some lifts than others. Therefore, use %1-RM shown in the table above only as a starting point for establishing your load. It is more important on lifts like the bench press and squat to challenge yourself within the repetition ranges than it is to be exactly within the %-1RM.

Appropriate rest between sets is an important factor in this program. Short rest periods during the hypertrophy and peaking phases result in accumulation of lactic acid, which is a stimulus for anabolic hormones and improves your ability to perform in spite of fatigue. Longer rest periods in the basic strength phase are designed to allow your body to restore ATP, so you have maximum energy in each set and can lift heavy enough to recruit the Type II muscle fibers. It is especially important to avoid rushing though workouts during the basic strength phase. If you find that you can recover in less time than two minutes, then increase the amount of weight you are lifting.

Adapt Periodization to Meet Your Needs

How you execute each phase, or whether you even use it, depends on your needs and the time of the year you are in. For example, you only need to use the sets and reps of the anatomical adaptation period if you haven't done a specific exercise for several months. Furthermore, during the season, you will probably not need a hypertrophy phase at all, because you will want to maintain your weight class. The program in Appendix B provides an example of how you might structure these phases to meet your needs during a year that incorporates a wrestling season that goes from November to March.

Strength Training and Increased Muscle Size

Some people mistakenly assume that lifting heavier weights for fewer sets won't increase their muscle size. This is false. Any amount of muscular overload will increase muscle size to some degree depending on your nutritional status and your training history. If you are just beginning a lifting program, the amount of muscle size increase in any given program is usually greater than if you have been lifting for several months. Therefore, if you have never lifted weights and start during wrestling season (and also begin eating more), you might notice an increase in your muscle mass. However, it is also possible to strength train throughout the season and stay within your weight class, unless you are growing rapidly.

Can You Get Stronger Without Getting Much Bigger?

When people train for strength and endurance at the same time, it is referred to as concurrent training. Research on concurrent training has shown that the muscle fibers of people who do both types of training at the same time don't get as big as the ones who do strength training without endurance training. This only happens in the muscles that are being worked for both strength and endurance, however. Performing the sprint workouts outlined in chapter 2 will probably be sufficient to minimize unneeded muscle size increases during the season. However, the best way to avoid getting too big when you are in season is to avoid taking in more calories than necessary. This should be easy, because you will be burning a lot more calories during in-season training.

IN-SEASON TRAINING: STRENGTH OR CIRCUIT?

Many wrestlers and their coaches make the mistake of transitioning from strength training to strength-endurance training too early in the season. In fact, some teams switch from lifting for strength to circuit training within the first weeks of practice. The irony of this is that the training volume associated with wrestling practices is much higher than what you may have been doing in the off-season and the sprints your coaches make you do at the end of practice should provide ample conditioning.

If you are in high school and your strength program is optimal, then you may be able to increase strength throughout the season. Think of how much better you will perform at the end of the season if you are in great shape and very strong.

Assuming the competitive part of your wrestling season goes from November to February or March, you should train for strength all the way though January. Don't transition to circuit training until about four weeks before you want to peak. If you are confident you will qualify for your state or national tournament, base your transition date off those dates, otherwise use your qualifying tournament as your target date. Use the Periodized Program Adapted to Wrestling on page 115 to design your training program to meet your individual needs.

KEEP STRENGTH TRAINING IN PERSPECTIVE

Strength training is a rewarding and fun activity. In fact, it can be addictive, because it can make you bigger, stronger and make you feel better about your appearance. However, it is only meant to supplement your wrestling training and increase your performance. If you allow yourself to get too caught up in training to get bigger muscles or to look better, then you may spend too much time in the weight room looking in the mirror and not enough time working on your wrestling technique. The training programs associated with body building and some of the extreme nutritional practices used by cosmetic fitness enthusiasts can have a negative impact on wrestling performance. You will have the rest of your life to focus on cosmetic fitness, but a limited amount of time to become the best wrestler you can be.

RECOMMENDED READING

Baechle, T. R. and R.W Earle. *Weight Training: Steps to Success,* 3rd ed. Champaign, IL: Human Kinetics. 2006.

Baechle, T.R., R.W. Earle, and D. Wathen. Resistance training. In: *Essentials of Strength Training and Conditioning,* 3rd ed. T.R. Baechle ed. Champaign, IL: Human Kinetics. 2008.

Hedrick, A. Training Greco-Roman wrestlers at the U.S. Olympic Training Center. *Strength and Conditioning* October, 1996.

Kraemer, W.J. et al. Compatibility of high-intensity strength and endurance training on hormonal and skeletal muscle adaptations. *Journal of Applied Physiology* 78:976-989. 1995.

Stone, M.H. and H.S. O'Bryant. *Weight Training: A Scientific Approach.* Minneapolis, MN: Burgess. 1987

Wathen, D, T.R. Baechle, and R.W. Earle. Periodization. In: *Essentials of Strength Training and Conditioning,* 3rd ed. T.R. Baechle ed. Champaign, IL: Human Kinetics. 2008.

PART TWO

Nutrition and
Weight Management

CHAPTER 7

Eat to Pin

I took my car in for an oil change a few days before our family was to leave for a long trip one summer. The mechanic told me the various grades of oil he had in stock and asked what I wanted. When I told him about our upcoming trip and asked whether it would be worth loading up with some high-tech oil (the stuff that's about triple the price of normal oils), he gave me an answer that I've often remembered. He told me that putting high-quality oil in a car is a commitment a person makes over the lifetime of the vehicle not just before taking a long drive.

You can make a lot of comparisons to fueling your body just like it was a high-tech machine. Good nutritional practices should be a life-long commitment, not just something you do during the wrestling season. Fortunately, you can achieve sound nutrition with a little knowledge of what your body needs. This chapter will give you an overview of the various nutrients needed and then show you how to estimate the number of calories you need.

WATER POWER

When scientists have considered whether life could exist on other planets, they determine, among other things, if there is any water available. All living things require water, which has important functions such as providing blood volume and regulating body temperature.

You've heard about being dehydrated and perhaps you've even experienced it to some degree. Dehydration can have serious consequences for health and performance. In fact, losing as little as 1% of your body weight from dehydration can make it difficult for you to keep cool during exercise. Losing three to five percent of your body weight without replenishing the losses, such as during a workout, can cause your heart to work harder.

Let's say you weigh 130 pounds. Have you ever lost two pounds in wrestling practice? That would put you a little above the 1% threshold for an increase in core temperature. How about cutting weight? If you've ever sucked five or six pounds in a few days to make weight, then your heart has probably done a little extra work.

The risks of dehydration are serious enough that wrestling governing bodies from the high school level to the international level have established rules to reduce the likelihood that athletes will participate in unsafe measures to make weight. Most of these changes came after the unfortunate (and unprecedented) deaths of three college wrestlers in a five-week period in 1997. In each case, the wrestler was trying to lose weight through methods of rapid dehydration.

How Much Water Do You Need?

For years people have said you need to drink six to eight glasses of water each day, but this fails to account for a person's body size or how much a person is losing through sweat. The two easiest ways to determine if you need to drink more are whether you are thirsty and the color of your urine. If you are thirsty or if your urine is yellow (it should be the color of lemon juice), you need to drink more.

Both of these methods have limitations. Experts say that you can be mildly dehydrated and not thirsty, and the color of your urine will be affected by vitamins and other supplements you might be taking. Nevertheless, thirst and urine color are still the most practical way to gauge your hydration status. If you're not thirsty, and your urine is the right color, you are probably not going to die. Furthermore, you will probably be sufficiently hydrated to perform well in practice or in matches—especially if you are making a conscious effort to stay hydrated.

There is one more thing you can do. Most of the weight certification processes involve testing your hydration, so the person that conducts that test will be able to tell you your hydration level. You might find it helpful to ask for a hydration test when you are NOT trying to modify your body weight. (There are also scales you can purchase, that will tell you your hydration status, just do the research to make sure the one you buy is accurate.) Drink enough fluids to meet the hydration guidelines that would allow you to pass the weight certification test. Remember what you weigh at the hydrated state and use thirst, urine color, and your body weight to help you make sure you are getting enough fluids. Hydration is actually the easy part of the nutrition equation.

"A Pint for Every Pound:" Replacing Fluid Losses

It can be difficult to stay hydrated during a workout in a warm environment such as a wrestling room with 30 athletes all clamoring for a few sips of water at the same time. Thus, you will need to replace your fluid losses as soon as possible after practice. The simplest strategy for doing this is to put back in what you lost by sweating.

If you are like many wrestlers, you may be in the habit of checking your weight before practice, which is an excellent habit for your hydration plan. Weighing yourself after practice will enable you to see how much weight you lost during the workout.

The phrase "a pint for every pound" is easy to remember. A pint is 16 ounces and a pound is 16 ounces. Replace what you lost in practice (or any other workout) plus a little more, because you will likely urinate before your cells and tissues are fully hydrated.

Advanced Hydration

You lose more than water when you sweat; you also lose the electrolytes sodium chloride and potassium. Fortunately, the adaptive mechanisms in your body will help you retain those electrolytes as you become accustomed to sweating. Furthermore, many people get more than enough sodium in their diets to compensate for losses through sweating. You can stock up on potassium by eating foods high in potassium such as potatoes, citrus fruits, and bananas and drinking your milk.

However, electrolyte replacement is only part of the hydration picture. When you workout, your body uses sugars for energy. The more intensely you exercise, like in wrestling practice, the more energy you use. As blood sugar drops, your body begins looking for ways to make new sugar, such as tapping into your hard-earned muscle tissue. (That's why you lose muscle in addition to fat when you starve yourself to make weight.)

Research using weight lifting workouts has shown that people who drank something that contained sugar were able to increase muscle tissue and recover (at the muscle fiber level) faster than people who drank plain water. This was due to the maintenance of blood sugar during the workout, so the body didn't turn on the catabolic hormones to use muscle for fuel. Another interesting finding was that adding a small amount of protein to the sugared drink increased the benefits. Over about three months (most of the length of your wrestling season) people that drank the sugar and protein concoction had better increases in lean muscle mass than the ones that drank only water or the ones that drank water with carbohydrate (like Gatorade) only.

GOOD	BETTER	BEST
Water	Sugared drink	Sugared drink with protein

Probably the best news is that the concoction the researchers used was something that tastes halfway decent. Basically, the sugar concentration was similar to Gatorade, which has about a 6% solution of sugar to water (6 grams sugar/100 milliliters water) and the protein content was a mixture of essential amino acids, which are easily obtained in most protein powders. The ratio of sugar to protein was 4 to 1—kind of like what you would get if you added protein to Gatorade. Accelerade is a commercial sports drink with a similar ratio, but you can make your own by following this recipe.

| At-Home Recipe for Carb-protein Drink ||
Laboratory Formula	Kitchen Measurement Equivalents
1000 ml water	One quart water
60 grams sugar	¼ Cup + 1 Tablespoon sugar
16 grams essential amino acids	4 teaspoons of a protein powder with the essential amino acids
Flavoring	Flavoring: Kool-Aid powder mixed according to directions

When I make this recipe, I use lemon juice concentrate for the flavoring (about ¼ to ½ cup per quart) and a vanilla-flavored powder called Premium Protein manufactured by EAS, which I buy at Costco. I've also used various flavors of Kool-Aid, but I keep coming back to the lemonade concentrate. This concoction works as a post-workout refresher as well. Some people drink chocolate milk, which has that four-to-one ratio of carbohydrate to protein.

If you'd prefer to go without the protein, you can create your own sports drink by a mixing 16 ounces of a sugared drink, like orange or grape juice, with 8 ounces of water and adding about 1/8 teaspoon of salt.

I sip on the carbohydrate-protein drink between sets of my super circuit workout. For that level of intensity, I can stomach it with no problems. However, I couldn't use it when I was running 400-meter sprints with a very short rest, but even plain water had no appeal, because I was gasping for breath. I had to wait until after the workout to rehydrate. This underscores the importance of being optimally hydrated before a training workout.

If your coach allows it, you should bring your own water or drink to practice. This will allow you to avoid the line at the drinking fountain and enable you to use a sports drink if you want. Here is a four-step plan to begin a workout hydrated and maintain (as much as possible) hydration during practice.

Hydration: Four-Step Plan

- Step 1: Drink 16 ounces of fluid two hours before practice
- Step 2: Check your weight before practice
- Step 3: Drink 6-8 ounces every 15 minutes of practice
- Step 4: Check your weight after practice and replace what you lost ounce per ounce plus an extra 8-12 ounces to account for urinary output

Keys to Rapid Absorption of Fluids

People previously thought that chilled fluids (on ice) were more rapidly absorbed than fluids at room temperature. Chilled fluids have a potential benefit of cooling you as they move down your throat, but the warm surface of your esophagus will rapidly warm the fluid before absorption takes place. If you are like me and you try drinking something cold too fast, you might get that "brain freeze" headache for a few seconds. Just experiment and find the temperature that you prefer.

It seems that volume, the amount of fluid that gets into the stomach at one time, has a greater influence on how fast it leaves the stomach than temperature. To a certain degree larger volumes are absorbed faster than small volumes. Therefore, drink about four or five swallows each time you get a drink rather than just a sip to "wet your whistle."

You should experiment with your hydration strategy after you get past the initial few weeks of practice. During the first few weeks of practice, if you are a little out of shape, nothing you try will feel very good, so that would not be the best time to judge what works. Experimenting also means trying things that you might not think will work at first. I was an athlete who had been afraid to drink a large volume of water, because I was told it would give me stomach cramps. Through my own experimentation I discovered that I could drink more than I would have thought (unless it is between sets of sprinting) without the problems I expected.

MACRONUTRIENTS: CARBS, PROTEIN AND FAT

All of the food you eat can be classified as carbohydrate, protein or fat. Because so much of our nutritional requirements come from carbohydrate, protein and fat, these are called macronutrients. Understanding these nutrients and how much you need to consume is the first step in creating a high-performance body and controlling your weight.

Carbohydrates

Carbohydrates (or "carbs") are sugars, which provide most of your energy during high-intensity exercise like a wrestling match. Carbohydrates should make up about 55-65% of your total caloric intake. Recommendation ranges account for different types of athletes. For example endurance athletes engage in steady exercise for long periods of time and can benefit from a high carbohydrate diet. You, as a wrestler, train hard, but you have intermittent bouts of high intensity work, so your requirements may be a little less.

Depending on size of the sugar molecule and arrangement of the carbon, hydrogen, and oxygen, which make up a carbohydrate, carbs can be various forms of simple sugars or complex carbohydrates. Digestion breaks down carbohydrate into glucose, which is how it is transported in the blood stream. When people talk about levels of blood sugar, they are referring to blood glucose.

Glucose is transported to muscle cells where it is stored as a larger molecule called glycogen. However, the glucose cannot get into the cells by itself—it's kind of like getting into a party without knowing the password. In the case of sugars, a hormone called insulin provides the password and helps the carbs get into the cells.

When blood sugar is high, a lot of insulin is released. People that are diabetic have a problem regulating their blood sugar levels for various reasons relating to how well their bodies can release insulin, but for most people the system works well. In fact, it works well enough that if you have a rush of glucose into the blood stream, from eating or drinking something with a lot of sugar, like pop, so much insulin is released that it rapidly clears the blood sugar. Ironically, this causes you to have low blood sugar.

Your brain uses blood sugar for fuel, so when the levels are low, it sends various signals throughout your body, one of which is to make you feel hungry for sweets and another is to break down muscle and fat for energy. If you eat another sweet food, the same process is repeated, but this time, when the blood sugar gets to a muscle cell, it will find a "no vacancy" sign, because, if you haven't been exercising, the muscle has most of the glycogen it needs. However, your fat cells are like a hotel that increases in size with the demand for occupancy, so the sugar will find a home there and will be stored as a fat.

Glycemic Index

The roller coaster of high and low blood glucose can be a problem if you are trying to maintain energy throughout the day. Having some degree of control over your blood glucose has implications for performance in sport as well. Scientists have been taking a hard look at something called the glycemic index (also called "GI"), which is a rating of foods in terms of how quickly they can raise blood sugar. You can use the internet or nutrition books to get more information about the GI of various foods.

Glycemic Index of Various Foods	
Higher	*Lower*
White Bread	Whole-grain Bread
Doughnut	Apple
Raisins	Orange Juice
Sugared pop	Lentils
Sports drinks like Gatorade	Milk
Carrots	Yogurt

Several things influence the GI of a food, such as how it is prepared and what other things you might be eating with it. If you eat a high-GI food with a fat or a protein, it will reduce the likelihood of a large spike in blood glucose compared to if you ate it alone. Also remember that the amount of the food that you eat will influence the response. You might eat a high-GI food like a carrot, for example, but the overall increase on blood glucose would be small, because you have consumed a small amount of food.

When you are at rest—studying, hanging out and doing light activities like household chores, you want to consume mostly low-GI foods. These foods will act like a time-release into your blood stream. They'll provide you with the energy you need. Furthermore, the constant level of blood sugar will keep your brain happy, so it won't send signals to break down your hard-earned muscle tissue for fuel.

On the other hand, you will want a high-GI food soon after a hard workout to replenish the stores of muscle glycogen that you used for energy during the workout. This doesn't mean you need to drink a case of pop or eat a box of candy bars. Drinking a sport drink, eating a bagel or another high-GI food will do the trick, especially if you follow up with a meal that includes low- and moderate-glycemic index foods afterwards.

Some people mistakenly think that if they are trying to lose weight that they shouldn't eat after the workout or that they should try to work out on an empty stomach to help them use more body fat for fuel. This doesn't really work, because of the signals your brain sends out to break down muscle, when your blood sugar is low. Ironically, the best strategy for losing body fat and maintain lean muscle mass is to keep a constant supply of blood glucose. This is one reason I suggest consuming some kind of a sports drink during your hard wrestling practices as I mentioned.

Here is my recommendation for using GI depending on what you are doing. Remember that the meal examples are just one of many things you could do. Sometimes people don't eat anything but the recommended meal. You should not consume the meal below indefinitely; use this as an example and strive for variety as you make healthful choices of your own.

Throughout the day
Mixed diet of low-, medium- and high-GI foods consumed with proteins and heart-healthy fats

Examples
Cereal, milk, fruits and vegetables, like tomatoes, avocadoes and potatoes eaten with proteins like chicken or fish.

Before two-hour practice or a workout
Consume low- or moderate-GI foods (mostly carbohydrate sources) about two hours before practice

Pre-workout meal (2-3 hours before)
Turkey sandwich on multi-grain bread, orange, low-fat yogurt, chocolate chip cookie, water or skim milk

During practice
Consume a mixture of water and sports drinks about 6-8 oz every 15 minutes

After practice
Have a high-GI snack

During-practice hydration plan
Alternate water and a sport drink every 15 minutes of your workout.

After practice
Watermelon chunks and a banana, followed by mixed diet meal within a few hours

Low-fat or low-carb diet for weight loss: which is better?

Traditionally, we've always thought the best way to lose weight was by combining a low-fat diet with an increase in aerobic exercise. New research is challenging these ideas. Insulin, the hormone that helps the sugars from carbs get into muscle cells, is also involved in how much fat your body breaks down and converts to energy. After you eat a carbohydrate source, your insulin levels are elevated, and your body is less likely to break down fats for energy. On the flip side, slight reductions in carbohydrate intake increase your body's reliance on the breakdown of fat for energy. This isn't to say that you shouldn't be eating carbs. As an athlete you need carbs for energy! However, you should make a conscious effort to reduce your consumption of simple sugars (like those found in candy) and look for low-glycemic choices when you are not as active.

Protein

Protein has been the center of diet controversy for years with people advocating both high- and low-protein diets. Later you will learn the most sensible recommendations, but for now let's consider why you need protein in your diet. You are one big unit of protein, which has other substances called bones that protect your body. Your cells, muscles and organs are comprised of protein, so consuming protein is critical to the growth and repair of these tissues.

Basically, the proteins you eat are composed of various amino acids. Amino acids are carried in the blood to the locations they are needed (like your muscle) and reassembled into body tissue. There are twenty amino acids that can be combined to create all of the proteins your body needs. Eleven of these amino acids can be formed by your body, but the nine listed below are essential amino acids, because they must be supplied in the diet.

Essential Amino Acids

Histidine	Isoleucine	Leucine	Methionine	Lysine
Threonine	Tryptophan	Valine	Phenylalanine	

Both plant products and animal products are sources of protein, but animal proteins are higher quality proteins because they supply all the essential amino acids (and in higher amounts) than plant proteins. A diet that contains no animal products (vegetarian diet) may still provide all the essential amino acids, but a person needs an understanding of which plant products have high protein values. Unless you are ethically opposed to consuming animal products, I recommend consuming a mixture of plant and animal products to meet your needs.

Now, how much protein do you actually need? Well, that depends on who you ask. Let's start with recommendations by the American College of Sports Medicine (ACSM). This organization is made up of nutritionists and exercise scientists who do laboratory research to determine how to best help athletes. Because their research must endure the scrutiny of many independent reviewers, their recommendations are taken seriously by organizations like the USDA and other big-time government agencies. Therefore, if these recommendations are different from what your friend, Biff, the bodybuilder tells you, then you might want to compare the credentials of the sources.

During the past several years, the ACSM and leading nutritionists have recommended that athletes consume between .5 and .8 grams of protein per pound of body weight. If you are strength training, restricting calories (cutting weight), or have recently increased your training volume, then you have an increased need for tissue repair and you probably can benefit from the higher end of the recommendation—about .8 grams per pound of your body weight. Another recommendation is that 12%-15% of your calories come from protein. This amount is considered to be safe and effective for meeting your protein needs.

Fat

Some people think that fats are bad, when, in fact, fats are extremely important in the diet. For one thing, fats are an excellent source of energy. By way of comparison consider that one gram of fat contains 9 calories of energy, whereas carbohydrate and protein contain only 4 calories per gram. Furthermore, fats are needed to make up important structures in cells and nerves, and they provide a lot of the energy you use when you are at rest. In fact, fats are even important when a person is trying to lose weight, because they help you feel satisfied longer.

Well, if fats are so important, then why is there such a fear of eating fat among some people? First of all, eating too much fat can make you fat and once you store fat, it is very hard to lose it. Tell me something I don't know, right? Secondly, not all fats are equal. Certain animal products (such as red meat) are high in the saturated fats that increase a person's risk for developing coronary artery disease.

For these reasons, no more than 30% of the calories in your diet should come from fat. If you are trying to lose weight, you might try to stay between 20-25%. However, don't go overboard and totally eliminate fat from your diet—even for short periods of time. Not only will you be missing an essential part of your diet, but consuming than 15% of your calories from fat may put you at risk for lowered testosterone production. Not cool!

MICRONUTRIENTS: VITAMINS AND MINERALS

Vitamins and minerals are needed in much lower quantities than carbs, proteins and fats, because they function in supportive roles. Some people mistakenly think that they can take increased amounts of vitamins or minerals and it will help them have more energy. This is not the case. Although vitamins and minerals help you use the energy in the foods you eat, but they do not make energy themselves.

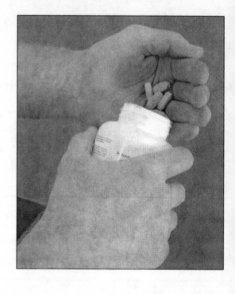

You may be most aware of micronutrients when you think of multi-vitamins and other supplements, but the reality is that a balanced diet will provide you with all the vitamins and minerals you need. The key here is that you have a *balanced* diet that contains enough calories for your needs. That can be problematic if you are cutting weight or you are not careful to include the major food groups in your meals.

Some people supplement with a multi-vitamin to ensure they get what they need. This is pretty common, and I would certainly recommend it, especially during times when your diet might be less than adequate. A multi-vitamin supplement, by a reputable manufacturer (you'll learn how to judge a supplement company in chapter eight) taken at the recommended dosages will not harm you, even if you are getting enough without the supplement.

Before running to the store to buy a multi-vitamin incorporate these six steps to do the best you can with your diet.

1. Follow the "5-a-day" rule. Consume five servings from the fruit and vegetable group each day. I know this can be hard, if you are not in the habit. I have a difficult time myself. If you eat a serving with breakfast, lunch and dinner, and then add one for a mid-morning and mid-afternoon snack you will get your five.

2. Consume colorful and fresh fruits and vegetables, which are higher in nutrient content, as much as possible.

3. Drink your milk (unless you have problems digesting dairy products). The calcium in milk is extremely important for healthy bones for males and females.

4. Use cast-iron cookware for preparing foods. As weird as it sounds, this will increase the iron content in your food.

5. Don't go overboard on salt. Most diets in the United States contain plenty of salt.

6. Choose whole grains over refined grains.

YOUR CALORIE NEEDS

Now that you have reviewed some of the basics, it's time to figure out how much you need to eat to meet your requirements. First, you'll estimate how many calories you are burning, then you will figure out how much of each of the macronutrients to consume. You should note that this activity will give you an only rough estimate of your needs.

Although it is not perfect, it works because you generally will not count calories every day. If you really want to get technical, you can do one of two things. The first is to visit the website mypyramid.gov which is sponsored by the USDA. This excellent site will help you estimate your energy needs, analyze your diet, and provide you with portion-sized recommendations for improvement.

An alternative to using this USDA program is to work with a registered and licensed dietician. Although it will be more expensive than the computer, you will get excellent results. I have been impressed at the enthusiasm of the nutritionists I have met, especially when they are working with athletes.

Estimating Your Energy Needs

Your caloric requirements are based on several factors, but the main ones are your body size and your activity level. Here is a simple chart to estimate your needs. Identify your average activity level, and multiply your body weight in pounds by the number of calories for that level.

Light activity refers to the effort of walking at a slow pace, cleaning house, playing golf or things like that. Moderate activity is a little harder and would include things like playing tennis, cycling, dancing or skiing. Heavy would be the effort you expend carrying something up a hill, playing soccer, and, of course, wrestling.

Estimated Caloric Needs		
	Male	*Female*
Activity Level	Calories per pound	Calories per pound
Light	17	16
Moderate	19	17
Heavy	23	20

Adapted with permission, from K. Reimers 2008, Nutritional factors in health and performance. In *Essentials of Strength Training and Conditioning*, 3rd., edited by T. R. Baechle and R. W. Earle for the National Strength and Conditioning Association (Champaign, IL: Human Kinetics), 223.

The limitation of the chart above is that it may be difficult to accurately estimate how active you are. When you're in the middle of the season or doing the training programs outlined in the appendix, your activity level is probably somewhere between the "moderate" and "heavy" classification. If you start by estimating your calorie needs at 20 per pound (for males), you can gauge your energy level and see how it influences your weight, then make adjustments as necessary.

Getting the Right Balance

Imagine a wrestler we'll call John who weighs about 145 pounds and is heavily active. He burns about 23 calories per pound or about 3,400 total calories. If we want to know how many calories of carbs, protein and fat John should be eating, we start by multiplying his total caloric requirement by the recommended percentages of each macronutrient, which were 55-65% (carb), and 12-15% (protein). This would give us a range of calories for carbohydrate and protein. Because John is training hard, he should probably be at the higher ends of the protein recommendations. However, he is not an endurance athlete, so he should be somewhere in the middle of the carbohydrate recommendations.

3,400 Total calories	Carb (60%) 2,050 calories	Protein (15%) 510 calories	Fat (25%) 840 calories

Nothing on paper is ever perfect in the real world, so adjust this by how you feel in terms of energy and by how your weight is affected.

Using the Food Guide Pyramid

As exciting as those calculations must have been for you (yes, I am kidding!), it is not practical to count calories on a daily basis. Instead you should use the food guide pyramid to help you in serving up your meals. As I mentioned before, mypyramid.gov is an excellent way to plan your meals. Recent updates to the food guide pyramid make it easy for anyone of any size or activity level to know the servings and portion sizes of each food group to include your diet on a daily basis.

RECOMMENDED READING

American College of Sports Medicine. Nutrition and athletic performance. *Medicine and Science in Sports and* Exercise 41(3): 709-731. 2009.

Antonio, J. Timing and composition of protein/amino acid supplementation. *Strength and Conditioning Journal* 30 (1): 44-44. 2008.

Clark, N. *Nancy Clark's Sports Nutrition Guidebook.* 2nd ed. Champaign, IL: Human Kinetics. 1997.

Ferrando, A.A., K.D. Tipton, and R.R. Wolfe. Essential amino acids for muscle protein accretion. *Strength and Conditioning Journal* 31(1): 87-92. 2010.

Volek, J., W.J. Kraemer, and J.A. Bush. Testosterone and cortisol in relationship to dietary nutrients and resistance exercise. *Journal of Applied Physiology* 82:49-54. 1997.

Williams, M.H. *Nutrition for Health, Fitness & Sport* 2nd ed. Boston, MA: WCB McGraw-Hill. 1999.

www.mypyramid.gov

Several years ago the following hypothetical situation was posed to a number of elite-level athletes: Suppose there was a special pill that, if you took it, would guarantee you an Olympic gold medal, but the pill would cause your death within a year. Would you take it? Over 50% of the responding athletes said yes!*

For years people have been promoting various diets, supplements, and fitness products. There is big money to be made in this area, but it is nearly impossible to keep informed about everything out there. Therefore, I'm not going to discuss specific diets or fitness products in great detail, but I am going to tell you how you can use your brain and common sense to separate truth from some of the crap you hear. You will probably notice that I will sound a little more skeptical, even cynical, in this chapter. This is not necessarily to attack people or their positions, but to demonstrate questions or thought processes that will help you to ask the critical questions as you evaluate products and claims.

FOOD SAFETY: IT'S ABOUT TRUST

Imagine yourself walking in an aisle of a grocery store that had canned foods. Suppose each can has a label that says the name of the food, but does not list any ingredients and there are no markings to indicate an expiration date. Would you be excited about buying the product or would you want a little more information? It probably depends on whether you are familiar with the name of the food and whether you trust that the grocery store has safe products.

*Michael Bamberger and Don Yaeger, "Over the Edge," *Sports Illustrated*, 14 April 1997, pp. 60-70.

Fortunately, in the United States, we can be reasonably assured that the food we buy in grocery stores is fairly safe, or at least any bad stuff in the food is at low enough levels that we aren't going to keel over immediately. Why do most people have this level of trust about buying food from a grocery store and then eating it? For one thing people have to eat...frequently! It would be unreasonable for everyone to have to test their own food for safety, so the government created the Food and Drug Administration (FDA) to provide rules and regulations for the production of products that people use, including foods. The FDA inspects farms and places where drugs are manufactured and many other things to ensure compliance with safe and ethical practices. Is the FDA perfect? Certainly not. Occasionally, there are cases where someone gets ill from a batch of food, but the incidence of this is very low considering the amount of food people eat.

EVALUATING SUPPLEMENTS

Supplements have increased in popularity and availability in recent years to the point that it is difficult for anyone to keep up with all the new products. However, if you are going to take something, you must accept that fact that it's your responsibility to do some investigation regarding the safety and effectiveness of what you are taking. Some supplements deliver on their claims. Others are a waste of money and some may even contain substances that can harm you. Here are a few things to consider when considering taking a supplement.

FDA Regulation

Unlike foods you buy in the grocery store, the FDA does not regulate supplements during their production. In 1994 the government passed the Dietary Supplement Health Education Act (DSHEA), which meant that supplement manufacturers are responsible for ensuring a product is safe before it is sold. Here are a few of the specific details of DSHEA:

- A manufacturer is not required to provide FDA evidence to prove safety or effectiveness before or after it markets its products.

- Labeling on the bottle must include a descriptive name of the product which says it is a supplement and the name and place of business of the manufacturer, packer, or distributor; a complete list of ingredients; and the net contents of the product

- A supplement label must have a "Supplement Facts" panel. This label must identify each dietary ingredient contained in the product.

- There are no rules that limit what the manufacturer can recommend as a serving size or the amount of a nutrient in any form of dietary supplements.

- Supplement manufacturers cannot make any claims that the supplement will cure a disease.

Does any of this mean that supplements will harm you? Not necessarily. If fact, most supplements are probably fine. But it still pays to do your homework.

What is the claim?

Most supplements will claim one or a combination of benefits. You need to determine if the claim makes sense. Muscle gain is a logical claim, especially if the supplement adds substantial calories to your diet. On the other hand, when you consume something, like a supplement, it adds something to your body—you are, after all taking it into your body. Normally, this would make you gain weight, but if the supplement is supposed to help you lose weight, then it is somehow screwing with your body's natural metabolic processes.

The same holds true for claims of increased energy. If you were starving and you ate some food it would increase your energy. However, if you did not get enough sleep, food is not going to pep you up, but a stimulant like caffeine will. Supplements containing ephedra have been pulled from the market because the stimulants harmed people. They were pulled AFTER people had died.

Who makes the claims?

To effectively sell something, a manufacturer needs a spokesperson that will have credibility to the consumer. In our society doctors are respected and trusted, so people with a doctor's credentials sometimes promote supplements. Unfortunately, even people with doctor's credentials are not always ethical. Usually the person acting to promote a product will receive some kind of money for their endorsement. A good "second opinion" to anything a doctor on TV might claim about a supplement is to ask your own health care provider what he or she thinks about a product.

Frequently, athletes or celebrities endorse supplements. These people are great spokespersons for supplements, because they generally look good and have achieved success. I know that I am influenced by how a person looks on a supplement label or in a magazine, and I also want to know the secrets of a successful person. However, athletes and celebrities may not have the credentials to make accurate claims about how a supplement works or what it might do for a person. In fact, they might not even use the supplement themselves.

Hawking Supplements with Hype!

Quality products speak for themselves. Think of the differences you might have noticed in television advertising for cars. Commercials for new cars are classy and cool, but the commercials run by some local dude who is selling used cars are full of hype and excitement. You can see the same thing comparing traditional medicines with supplements. Supplements have infomercials that drag on forever repeating the same message in different ways, and promises that the product will do many things for you. On the other hand, commercials for medicines that have been shown to work do not need all the hype.

What are the ingredients?

Frequently, supplement labels will list some studies that were performed to determine the effectiveness of the product. Even this is not a guarantee of the effectiveness. Some research is crap. The best supplement research is performed by people who are completely independent of the manufacturer. Sometimes the research on supplements is performed by the companies that make the stuff. As a critical consumer, you can see the problem with this. Unfortunately, it is often difficult to determine whether the researcher was truly independent of the manufacturer. However, most of the stuff published in scientific journals would meet these qualifications. Your science teachers could probably help you figure out if a study reported on a science label came from a reputable source.

Are the substances in the product safe?

A supplement that contains ingredients found in food, such as the stuff in Gatorade, is probably not going to hurt you. Remember, however, that supplements may recommend serving sizes that are above what you need. These could have the potential to do you harm. For example, fat soluble vitamins can be toxic in too high a dosage, so it is important to make sure the serving sizes are in accordance with recommended amounts.

I am reluctant to be among the first people to try anything. Before I experiment with a supplement, I watch other people use it for a few years…kind of like how the kings had the food tasters eat something first to see if it would kill them. Kind of morbid, I know! In the short term, perhaps the stuff in supplements will do little or no harm, but one never knows what long-term usage can do to your body. Ephedra was used in various forms and throughout the world for years, so taking a supplement containing ephedra may not have frightened some people. Unfortunately, people did die after using products containing the stuff.

Some athletes might argue that if you wait awhile to take a supplement until it appears to be safe, then you will miss the opportunity for the competitive edge it might have provided. There is certainly that risk, however, most of the products that clearly provide any athletic advantages are quickly banned anyway. Even caffeine has established limits, and athletes who consume more than the limit will test positive for the substance on a drug test in some sports.

How much does the product cost per serving?

Amino acids in various amounts are the key ingredients in protein powders. However, you get the same nutrition from various sources of high quality proteins at a much cheaper price. What you pay for with supplements is their convenience. For many people the extra cost is not worth the convenience. If you are able to work out your schedule to allow you to get the majority of your nutrition from traditional food sources it will save you money in the long run.

Is supplementation really necessary?

In other words, if your diet provides enough nutrients, will adding more of the "active" nutrient via supplementation give you added benefit? You can spend a lot of money if you buy a supplement for six months or a year. Before dropping a bunch of money into a supplement that you might not need, spend a few a few hours with a nutritionist who will evaluate your diet and give you suggestions. The scary thing is that you might discover you don't need to supplement. What will you do with the money you save?

Consider This...

Here are a few suggestions to keep in mind as you evaluate supplements:

- Claims of "all natural ingredients" do not necessarily mean safe. Poison ivy is a "natural" substance. What would happen if it was used in an analgesic cream?

- A patented product means very little. When something is patented it is not tested for safety or effectiveness, it has only been evaluated and shown to be unique compared to other patented things. In the case of foodstuffs, they do not have to be evaluated by the FDA to get a patent.

- Watch out for quick fixes. Remember that matter can neither be created nor destroyed. Gaining weight and losing weight involves moving matter on and off your body. Hormones regulate these metabolic processes. Speeding up these processes often disrupts hormone balances.

- Claims that seem too good to be true...ARE too good to be true.

SUPPLEMENTS THAT MAY WORK

Many supplements actually deliver on the claims that are made. If a supplement proves to be effective (and safe), then it is important to determine if it will benefit you as a wrestler. First of all, you need to think about the physiological needs of wrestling.

During the match you need to be strong and you need to perform in spite of high levels of lactic acid build-up. You also need to be able to control your weight. Although there are several supplements that can provide various benefits, I will focus on the four supplements that might provide a benefit to you as a wrestler and those which appear to have a low potential for injury.

Creatine

Creatine can be found naturally in your body—it's synthesized primarily in the liver. You can consume creatine by eating red meats and fish. It is an important part of the ATP-PC system, because it can help rebuild ATP when you are working hard. Greater intramuscular amounts of creatine (the PC part of the reaction) can help delay fatigue during high-intensity activities like sprinting, wrestling or lifting weights. You can go at maximum intensity for longer. This might mean adding one more muscle-building repetition to a set in the weight room or pummeling a little harder for a takedown on the wrestling mat. There have been many research studies that have show that creatine is effective for improving strength performance.

Many supplement manufacturers produce creatine and the usual recommendation is to take about two grams per day. Some recommendations call for a loading does of 20 grams per day for five days, followed by two grams a day thereafter. These recommendations don't account for differences in body size between people, so I prefer dosages that are adjusted for body weight. In this case if you wanted a loading dose you would multiply your body weight in pounds by .136 and if you were using a maintenance dose you would take 1/10 of the loading dose.

Typical Creatine Recommendations	
Loading phase dosage:	Weight in pounds x .136 Example: 150 lbs x .136 = 20.4 grams
Maintenance phase dosage:	Weight in pounds x .0136 Example 150 lbs x .0136 = 2.04 grams

Taking creatine with a high-glycemic index carbohydrate increases the ability of creatine to enter the muscles cells where it is needed. Using a loading dosage for five days can fill your muscle cells with creatine faster than using a maintenance dose, but after about 4 weeks the levels will be the same whether you load or not. I don't recommend using a loading dose during the season. One of the side effects of creatine usage at both dosage levels is weight gain, some of which is due to water retention. If you are trying to maintain or cut some weight this added water will not make things any easier.

There have been many reports of negative side effects associated with the use of creatine such as muscle cramps, stomach and intestinal problems, and others. However, research has not yet shown that creatine is likely to cause these problems when taken in recommended dosages. You should realize, however, that we still don't know what taking creatine every day for several years could do to you. Therefore, you should factor that into your decision as to whether or not to use it.

Beta-alanine

One of the limiting factors as to how hard you can push yourself when you are wrestling is the build-up of lactic acid. The hydrogen ion in lactic acid disrupts the processes that make muscle contraction possible. Carnosine, which is found in your muscles, actually helps to buffer the lactic acid and allows you to work harder. Two amino acids, beta-alanine and histidine, help your muscles make carnosine. Studies have shown that supplementing with beta-alanine improved subjects' work capacity at intensities similar to what you need for wrestling.

Beta-alanine is not the only substance that can buffer the hydrogen in lactic acid. Plain old baking soda (called sodium bicarbonate) will also do it. Unfortunately, the amount of baking soda you need to eat is enough to cause most people to have severe stomach cramps and diarrhea...probably not what you want in the middle of a dual meet!

Typical recommendations for beta-alanine range from 1.6-6.4 grams per day. Usually these doses are about 0.8 grams taken every three hours. The reason for breaking up the doses is because bolus doses (taking a bunch all at once) of 3.2 grams caused most people to have irritating, allergy-like symptoms. This was due to the release of histidine during the reactions that create carnosine. Although the symptoms aren't toxic, they are uncomfortable. Subjects taking smaller doses separated by three hours didn't have the irritating responses. Although research supports performance improvements when subjects have used beta-alanine, it may not be worth the irritation that you might experience.

Caffeine

Caffeine is probably the most commonly used stimulant in the world. People love caffeine, and for good reason. There are numerous quality research studies to show that caffeine is associated with short-term improvements in many types of performance.

Endurance athletes appear to benefit the most from caffeine use, but there are a few studies that suggest it might help trained power athletes. Probably the best benefit to you would be to help increase your arousal before a workout or competition. You probably notice that your performance is better on the days you feel more alert and ready to rumble.

The amount of caffeine in a cup of coffee or a can of caffeinated pop may be enough to help some people, but people who habitually consume the stuff may need more to feel the effect. Although there are several caffeine-containing energy drinks on the market, the performance benefits are best when a person takes caffeine in a tablet form. Research has shown that caffeine improves performance when a person consumes about 3-9 milligrams per kilogram of their body weight, which is about 1.4-4 milligrams per pound. Both the International Olympic Committee and the NCAA have established limits to the amount of caffeine athletes can legally have in their system. The IOC has set the limit at 12 micrograms of caffeine per milliliter of urine in a sample and the NCAA allows up 15 micrograms. These limits are pretty generous—a 170-pound athlete would have to drink about 5 or 6 regular cups of coffee to reach the IOC's limit.

Protein

How about good old protein? Don't forget that the amino acids in protein are the building blocks of muscle. If you are not getting adequate protein in your diet, then I recommend supplementation. In fact, of the supplements I've written about, protein is the most important. When you are trying to gain weight or if you are restricting calories you need greater amounts of protein than when you are not training. You can increase your protein intake by eating a few extra servings of foods rich in high-quality proteins that supply the essential amino acids.

The time of day that you consume protein is important as well. When you consume protein before right before a workout, you get a much better anabolic response and greater delivery of the amino acids to the muscle cells than when you eat protein right after a workout. However, eating some kind of protein immediately after the workout has better muscle building responses than if you wait an hour. In both cases, you can see that a protein supplement would be beneficial, because it would be rather difficult to consume whole foods at these times. Liquid nutrition, such as a protein shake, would probably be better.

Most of the research suggests that a range of 5-15 grams of essential amino acids provides the benefits. Whey protein tends to be faster at getting the amino acids to the muscles than casein, so that would be a better choice before and after your workouts. If you add some carbohydrate, such as table sugar, it will increase the benefit. Use a 4:1 ratio of carbohydrate to protein.

TO BUY OR NOT TO BUY...THAT IS THE QUESTION

Whether you choose to consume supplements is a personal choice. It appears that more people supplement than they did twenty years ago. It gives me a lot of pride in being a wrestler when I consider that wrestling and the martial arts have not been caught up in the doping scandals on the same levels that have occurred in other sports. As I mentioned previously, most of the supplements that give you a distinct advantage are banned. Furthermore, you have small guarantees they are safe.

I am not convinced you need to take supplements to be successful. In fact, I would be interested to see how many of the various state or national champions in the United States regularly consume a supplement that is marketed to enhance performance. Most of the champions I have known were more focused on working hard than keeping up with the hottest performance-enhancing substances.

RECOMMENDED READING

Eitzen, D. S. and G.H. Sage. Social problems and North American sport: Violence and drugs. *Sociology of North American Sport* 5th ed. Dubuque, IA: WCB Brown and Benchmark. 1993.

Graham, T.E. and L.L. Spriet. Performance and metabolic responses to a high caffeine dose during prolonged exercise. *Journal of Applied Physiology* 78: 867-884, 1995.

Harris, R.C. et al. The absorption of orally supplied beta-alanine and its effect on muscle carnosine synthesis in human vastus lateralis. *Amino Acids* 30:279-289, 2006.

Hoffman, J.R. Caffeine and energy drinks. *Strength and Conditioning Journal* 32(1): 15-20, 2010.

Hultman, E. K. et al. Muscle creatine loading in men. *Journal of Applied Physiology* 81:232-237, 1996.

Tipton, K. D. et al. Ingestion of casein and whey proteins result in muscle anabolism after resistance exercise. *Medicine and Science in Sports and Exercise* 36: 2073-2081, 2004.

Wilson, J.M. et al. Beta-alanine supplementation improves aerobic and anaerobic indices of performance. *Strength and Conditioning Journal* 32(1): 71-78, 2010.

www.fda.gov/Food/DietarySupplements/ConsumerInformation/ucm110417.htm#safe

CHAPTER 9

Wrestling with the Scale

If you begin wrestling at five years of age and wrestle on a varsity squad through high school and college, you will end up weighing in for competitions approximately 300 times. And that is a conservative estimate! Making weight the right way impacts your entire career. Before we get started on how to properly make weight, let's look at some facts about weight loss and wrestling.

As you might guess, most wrestlers lose some weight for competition. A survey of 2,500 Michigan wrestlers in the late 1990s revealed that two thirds had lost weight for competition and of these over half had lost an average of six pounds in the five days before competitions. Maybe this describes you.

To people unfamiliar with rapid weight loss, this sounds pretty horrible, especially when people talk about the "crazy" methods wrestlers have used to lose weight, such as skipping meals, working out in saunas and other things. Unfortunately, these stories paint a worse picture than may actually exist. While it is true that in a five-week period in 1997 three college wrestlers died while trying to make weight, the numbers of weight loss injuries are surprisingly low given the high numbers of wrestlers that do it—to say nothing of the boxers and martial arts competitors who do the same things. Furthermore, the fact that the wrestling deaths occurred in such a short period creates a question of whether additional circumstances may have been involved.

Sometimes people are tempted to do things because it seems like everyone else is doing it. In this case, you may have been tempted to try some methods of weight loss because you have seen other successful wrestlers using them. Before you decide to do something because it appears so common, consider what the Michigan wrestlers reported in terms of their weight loss habits.

About half of them restricted food during a week's period of time, and about 30% skipped meals. Thirty-five percent restricted fluid intake, but only two percent used laxatives or threw up to control their weight in a typical week. About 11% said they used a rubber or plastic suit. (Nowadays, using plastics suits, saunas and other methods of rapid dehydration are prohibited.)

Clearly, not everybody is doing crazy things, and you don't have to either. I would like to tell you to never lose weight and to compete at your normal body weight, but that has been shown to be unrealistic. Furthermore, thousands of wrestlers have proven that you can safely lose weight gradually and that there are times when you can safely lose weight rapidly. The key is to do it correctly and with a sensible game plan.

PICKING THE RIGHT WEIGHT CLASS

I'm not going to tell you what weight you should wrestle. Even if I saw the results of your weight certification tests, I could not tell you what weight is right for you. I could tell you what weight you could safely make and how long it should take to get there, but what goes into the day-to-day grind of getting down to weight is altogether different.

Attitude is Everything!

You must have courage to be a wrestler. And this courage includes having the attitude that you will take on anybody of any size. If you have ever been in a fight, did you ask your opponent to weigh-in first? Imagine saying this, "I'm mad at you and I'm going to tear you apart, but before we begin, could I get you to step on the scale for a moment..."

Now, I'm not advocating fighting, but my point is that if you have ever been in a situation like that, you used more of your "fight-or-flight" instinct than a scale to determine what you would do. If the other person was *about* your size, then you probably chose to fight instead of run away. I call this the "sandlot-size-up." Why can't we have the same attitude about picking a weight class?

Years ago, I helped coach an athlete I'll call Sam, who felt he was too small to wrestle in the 142-pound weight class. He insisted he needed to be in the 134-pound class, where he struggled to make weight and often had no energy to win matches. A situation developed where the NCAA changed the weight classes (the wrestler's deaths mentioned earlier) and implemented rules to establish minimum allowable wrestling weights. Sam's certification put him all the way up at the 149-pound weight class. He changed his attitude and decided to focus more on being a tough wrestler than a weight cutter and ended up placing in the NCAA Division II national tournament the next season.

Thus, the first step in picking the right weight class is to have the right attitude about your wrestling. If you are afraid you cannot win matches at a higher weight class, then you will probably not do much better at a lower one. In the days before the college weight loss rules, it was common for wrestlers to compete at higher weight classes for most of the season and then drop to their chosen weight in the weeks before the NCAA championships. I noticed that many of the All-Americans and national champions who used this approach also won most their matches at the higher weight class as well.

Weight Cutting is Not Always the Solution

If your team is kind of average and you cannot beat the guys at your weight when you are a freshman or sophomore, it probably means that you have a lot of improvement to make in your technique before you try to cut weight. If you stay at the higher weight class, you can put more effort into skill development and strength training activities, which will benefit you more in the upcoming years. There is also a good chance that you can eventually beat the person at your weight class anyway, especially if he is somewhat average himself.

Remember, you can always go up in weight as well. In my senior season the high school state finals at my weight class featured a wrestler whom few people had heard about until that year. He was on a strong team and as a sophomore had wrestled varsity, but in his junior season he could not beat the wrestlers from the 132-pound weight class through the 167-pound weight class. He ended up wrestling in the 185-pound class for that season, where he had a marginal record, but was able to focus all his efforts on wrestling, not weight cutting. The following year he wrestled at his natural weight of 145 pounds where he had an outstanding season and placed second in the state.

When to Lose Weight

Sometimes losing weight is the right decision. Obviously, if you are fat, then you can lose weight. Part of the weight certification process will estimate your body fat. If you are above 7% fat, then you can be approved to shed some pounds.

If you are short for your weight class, then dropping to a lower division might help you as well. Some people think you cut weight to be strong for your weight class. Actually, you cut weight to be big (tall) for your weight class. The extra reach of being tall makes it easier to get to an opponent's legs and control him or her on the mat.

Finally, there are many situations where wrestlers drop to a lower weight class to increase their chances of winning the state or NCAA tournament. This is certainly a worthy goal. If you are legitimately in that category of ability, then go for it. But always counsel with your coaches and your parents who can help you to identify your realistic abilities.

I don't know if I would be tempted to cut weight to earn a low place (5th or below) in the state tournament, unless I was a senior. If you are good enough to be close to placing, then you are just as likely to place with hard work, and if you are that good as an underclassman, you will likely achieve that goal in the upcoming years.

DAY-TO-DAY EATING

Dieting and Dining

If you have high aspirations for wrestling success, then you must be dedicated to good eating habits throughout the year. Any time you put on excess body fat, you create more work and suffering for yourself in the future when you have to take the weight off. Fortunately, you don't have to suffer to eat healthy and keep your weight where it needs to be. The suggestions you are about to read will not only make it easier to get to your lowest possible weight, they are a foundation for healthful eating throughout your life.

The biggest problem with weight control in the U.S. is that most of us are just hogs, plain and simple. If you've ever seen a pig eat, you will know what I am talking about. They dive in after their food, taking no time to enjoy it or the company of the swine around them. In the U.S. we are the same way. We eat like there's no tomorrow, as if we are afraid every meal will be our last for a long time and we need to stock up on calories. Obviously, this isn't true, because most Americans are rarely more than 30 minutes from a source of nutrition and our houses have refrigerators that are within mere feet. Some of this is driven by our fast-paced lifestyles. Here is a fascinating conversation between an Italian and an American that illustrates two different attitudes about eating:

"The problem with you Americans," said the Italian "is that you don't like to eat."

"What do you mean, we don't like to eat?" came the reply. "We are all overweight."

"No, no," the Italian continued, "you eat, but you don't savor it. Your culture is so concerned with worries about being overweight that you feel guilty about the things you eat and you don't enjoy them. When Italians eat we make a big meal and the family comes over. We get fed physically, emotionally and socially.

"Americans eat in the car and when they are doing other things. You get filled physically, but not in other ways, and you eat more to compensate."

Can you relate to this? How many times have you snacked all day, and then at supper time sat down to eat because you felt like it was time to eat again? There is a difference between dieting and dining. The dieting approach focuses on all the things you should cut out of your diet and leaves you feeling dissatisfied. Rather than trying to eliminate everything from your diet all at once, start with your dietary culprits. These are things that add calories to your diet, but don't provide you with enjoyment. For some people this might be snacking on candy while studying, but not even enjoying the candy, because their mind is thinking about something else. In other words, the enjoyment you receive is not worth the excess calories you are consuming.

On the other hand, you should dine. Dining means that you take time to anticipate and enjoy what you are eating. For example, a small bowl of ice cream with family and friends will satisfy you, because you are feeding yourself physically, emotionally, and socially, but you will never get enough of mindless snacking, because you can never get enough of something you don't need.

Dining Delicacies vs. Dietary Culprits

Hopefully, the majority of your diet is healthful, but, if you are like most people, there are things you regularly eat that don't measure up to what constitutes good nutrition. I call these my dietary culprits. A culprit is something where the level of satisfaction you get isn't worth the amount of junk you are putting in your body. On the other hand, a dining delicacy meets your needs and you can be satisfied with a little bit. On paper, they might look the same in terms of their nutritional value, but the difference is the satisfaction you get when you are eating them. Here are some of my personal examples:

Cuprit: cheese—any kind! Some people go to the bar after work. I go to the refrigerator and pull out a block of cheese. If it was a good day, I celebrate by shaving off ¼ of a pound. Sometimes I eat it after a bad day to give myself a little pick-me-up. The problem is that after the first slice, I can't taste it anymore, because I am talking to my wife or my mind is on other things. In three minutes I can wolf down more calories than I can burn off in a twenty-minute workout!

Delicacy: egg nog. Yeah, I know, I'm kind of a holly jolly guy. But the fact is that I sip this stuff pretty gingerly even during the holidays. And mine is alcohol free, so that's not the reason for my self control. I drink this with my family, and because it satisfies, I don't need to drink that much at one time.

Try the following exercise to determine the difference between your dining delicacies and the dietary culprits that invade your life during a typical three-day period.

First, write the name of the food and when you eat it or what you are doing when you eat it. Then rate it on a scale of 1-5 (with five being highest) for both the satisfaction it gives you and how much conscious attention you are giving to its taste while you are eating it. Finally check the box for whether it is a delicacy or a culprit.

Food	Activity	Satisfaction	Attention	Delicacy	Culprit
				(Check one)	
		1 2 3 4 5	1 2 3 4 5		
		1 2 3 4 5	1 2 3 4 5		
		1 2 3 4 5	1 2 3 4 5		
		1 2 3 4 5	1 2 3 4 5		
		1 2 3 4 5	1 2 3 4 5		
		1 2 3 4 5	1 2 3 4 5		
		1 2 3 4 5	1 2 3 4 5		

Well, what do you think? Are there any things on your list that ended up being culprits, which surprised you? Perhaps there are a few things that you would have considered culprits, but are, in fact, delicacies for you. The key here is not to eliminate every unhealthful food from your diet. It is to set some realistic expectations for yourself with regard to those unhealthful foods.

Anything that you eat without thinking about it can be reasonably eliminated and you won't miss it. Maybe you eat Pop Tarts while you are studying or drink pop while you are working at your summer job. If you can eliminate these or substitute with better choices, then do it. You will find out soon enough if it was truly a culprit.

Continue to enjoy your delicacies. Use them as a reward for things you have accomplished. But don't eat them every day; if you do, they will no longer hold as much enjoyment for you and they will become culprits. Anticipate them and savor them slowly. A large piece of pie is no more satisfying than a small one, if it takes you the same amount of time to eat it.

If you have written that everything on this list gives you a lot of satisfaction and you always give them a lot of attention, then making necessary diet changes will be a little tougher for you. When you find it difficult to make the sacrifices to eat right, you must focus your thoughts on your wrestling goals. Eating is a huge part of the human experience, but it's not the only thing. Achieving your wrestling goals far outweighs anything on your food list that makes it harder to reach those goals.

Here are a few things you can do to keep your dining delicacies from becoming dietary culprits.

- Serve yourself up: Don't eat anything right out of the bag or the box. How do you know when to stop?

- Don't eat while standing. It's too easy to get distracted and do other things.

- Avoid late-night snacking. It's not so much that it's a bad time to eat. It is what you eat that causes problems. After all, when was the last time you reached for some carrot sticks at 10 p.m.?

CUT WEIGHT THE EASY WAY

If you have been diligent in keeping your weight under control and you have picked the appropriate weight class to begin with, then you should always be within about a day's striking distance of your competition weight. My college days were before the weight certification rules, which banned the use of saunas and plastic suits. Some guys, who weren't eating much and had to cut a lot of water weight, did not have the strength to wrestle a hard practice. As a result, we had days during the week that were "make weight" days.

Typically, if we competed on a Saturday, we could weigh-in sometime on Friday, so Thursday would be a make weight day, which was a short practice followed by guys working on their own to get their weights down. I didn't cut a lot of weight, so if I had two days before competition, I would usually either do a hard air dyne workout, like the one described in chapter two, or lift weights. Over the course of the season, this added up to about 10 days of extra conditioning and strength training that I would not have had, if I had been donning the plastics and working out. I was able to do this because my weight was usually within five or six pounds of my weight class the day before the weigh-in and about two or three pounds before I went to bed.

I knew from experience what I could eat the night before the weigh-in and how much weight I could lose at night as I slept. Most of the time I would eat a salad without dressing before bed, and then I would go for a run in the morning. Because I usually ran or did some conditioning most mornings, this wasn't any extra work. As I returned from the run and while I was still hot, I would often put on a plastic suit or ride a stationary bike in the sauna, but it usually didn't take more than 15 minutes. After the weigh-in, I would eat a meal and I felt fine. Basically, I just took advantage of timing my workout activities to cut the weight.

You can only do this if you are cutting a reasonable amount of weight and you keep track of how much weight you lose doing various things. Here are the three critical times to weigh yourself to get the information you need:

1. Before and after each wrestling workout.
2. Before going to sleep and after you wake up.
3. Before and after any other conditioning or strength training workout wherein you do not drink much during the training session.

I did this almost every day during each season in high school and college, so I always knew what I weighed, and I never had any trouble making weight. When I was in high school, there were times when I would weigh myself before and after doing things like mowing our lawn. My reasons were not so much that I was fanatical about it; I just wanted to gather as much information as possible, so I knew what to expect when it came time to cut the weight. In fact, understanding my body enabled me to make weight without being stressed out all the time.

Here are some things you can do to maximize your safety and preserve muscle mass you have worked to develop.

Cardio and the "Fat-burning" Zone

You may have heard that you should exercise at a low intensity if you want to burn body fat and lose weight. This is true—to a point. When you exercise at low intensities, a large percentage of your energy comes from fat. As your intensity increases, you rely more on the breakdown of sugars for energy. However, there are two problems with wrestlers training at low intensity to lose body fat. The first is that you burn fewer calories each minute in the so-called "fat-burning" zone than you do training harder, so it takes a lot longer. Fat loss over time depends a lot more on the overall number of calories you've burned and a lot less on whether they were fat calories or carb calories. Secondly, as a wrestler, you need to condition yourself at the same intensity you compete. Doing endless hours of low-intensity training is not a productive use of your time and may lead to overtraining in the long run. The bottom line is that you should burn your calories with high intensity interval training and eat right to lose the fat.

Avoid Dramatic Weight Swings

When I was about 12, I talked with an older wrestler who had been a high school state place winner, who told me that he would make weight for a Saturday tournament, eat all day Sunday, and then start cutting again on Monday. Even though I was impressed with his success, it seemed like his methods were a little odd. However, the beginning of my freshman year in high school I fell into a little of the same habit of pigging out after weigh-in or a competition, and then having more weight to cut later.

During my sophomore season, I tried an experiment after cutting about seven pounds to make my weight. Instead of pigging out the day after the competition (and gaining back the 11 pounds I had originally lost), I just ate enough to be satisfied. This means I didn't eat until I was full, I just ate slowly and until I was no longer hungry. When I came to school on Monday, my weight was within about 5 pounds of where I would compete the following Saturday and I was able to eat more throughout the entire week.

Don't Be a Jerk About it...

In my years of wrestling, I've seen a lot of weight cutting crybabies. These dudes make the lives of everyone around them miserable, because they happen to be cutting some weight. I've seen them treat their mothers, wives or girlfriends badly during "that time of the season." Frankly, it appears to be the less successful wrestlers who do this. Perhaps it's because they know that making weight is the only battle associated with the competition they will win and they want to draw as much attention as possible to their suffering to do so. By contrast, the best wrestlers make weight quietly and get their attention in competition.

Keep the Muscle: Strength Train While Weight Cutting

Earlier you learned that strength training causes your body to release anabolic hormones, which build your muscle tissue. When your blood sugar is low, your body releases catabolic hormones, which break down muscle and use it for energy. That's why people tell you that when you starve yourself, you will lose muscle in addition to fat.

Unfortunately, I've never met a wrestler, except a heavyweight, who didn't skip a meal or two to make weight. However, if you continue to lift weights during the weight cutting process, you will stimulate the release of anabolic hormones that will help you to keep the muscle mass you have. Strength training will not prevent the loss of some muscle mass, but it will be stimulating anabolic processes on some level at the same time.

The best exercises are power cleans, deadlifts and squats, which all activate large amounts of muscle tissue and give you the greatest likelihood of stimulating anabolic hormone release. The workout below fits the bill.

Exercise	Sets	Reps	Intensity	Rest
Power Clean or Deadlift	3	5	85%-90% 1-RM	1 min.
Lunge	2	4	10-RM weight	1 min.
Bent-over Row	2	6	8-RM weight	1 min.
Incline DB bench press	2	5	85-90% 1-RM	1 min.

EATING ON COMPETITION DAY

Once you've made weight, you need to get some energy back in your system. Here are a couple of ideas for pre-match meals.

Weigh-in 1 hour before competition	Weigh-in 2 hours before competition
6-8 oz of orange Gatorade 4 oz fruit cup	12-16 oz of Gatorade (more if you have time) ½ bagel One orange
6-8 oz grape PowerAde 1 medium banana	12-16 oz of Gatorade ½ peanut butter and jelly sandwich One apple

I was always a little nervous when I was at competitions, especially in high school. I found it beneficial to get away from the competition area when I was trying to eat. If I had a friend to talk to, it helped take my mind off the competition and it was easier to eat. Once I got the first match under my belt, in the case of a tournament, I was better able to tolerate food.

Don't be afraid if you cannot eat much before your first match. A car doesn't run any better on a full tank of gas than on one that's half full, and you will be just fine if you are able to at least get about eight ounces of Gatorade and a little starch like bread. If you find that you have trouble eating anything on a competition day, then you might consider wrestling at a higher weight class, which will require less weight cutting and allow you to have more energy coming into the competition.

Do the best you can to eat right on competition day, but don't let your food become a source of added stress for you. After I graduated from college, I wrestled in a tournament with the team I was coaching. I wasn't the least bit nervous about the competition, and, after I made weight, I was in the mood for some McDonald's breakfast burritos with hot sauce. After polishing off about five of them, I had one of the best tournaments of my life!

RECOMMENDED READING

Kimpel, S.S. Feeding the tiger cubs. *Wrestling USA* October, 2003.

Kiningham, R.B, and D.W. Gorenflo Weight loss methods of high school wrestlers. *Medicine and Science in Sports and Exercise* 33 (5): 810-813. 2001.

Kraemer, W. J. et al. Influence of exercise training on physiological and performance changes with weight loss in men. *Medicine and Science in Sports and Exercise* 31: 1320-1329. 1999.

PART THREE

College
Preparation

CHAPTER 10
So You Want to
Wrestle in College

So you want to wrestle in college. Do you have what it takes athletically, academically, and character-wise to succeed in wrestling at the next level? Answering these questions will require you to analyze your motives.

First of all, why do you wrestle now? Do you love the thrill of competition or do you like the recognition that comes from being an athlete? Perhaps you are addicted the feeling you have after a hard conditioning workout. More than likely your motives are a combination of several things that make wrestling meaningful to you.

Recently, I've come to understand the importance of a person's motives in terms of how likely it is that a person will achieve his or her goals. The more intrinsic a person's motives—that is, driven by desires to do something independent of rewards or recognition from other people—the more likely the person is to continue the activity in spite of external changes. On the other hand, a person who has extrinsic motivation tends to put a lot of emphasis on things like recognition and awards.

For example, imagine a wrestler I'll call Joe. Joe is a high school senior who loves wrestling. He loves going to the tournaments and looking people in the eye after he wins a tough match. He likes having his parents and his girlfriend watching him compete and talking with them between his matches. Joe also likes to practice; in fact he is one of the better guys on the team, so he gets most of the takedowns and usually wins his practice matches. However, it wasn't always so good for Joe. Two years ago, he almost quit the team, because he had never made the varsity squad. His coach suggested that he do some extra conditioning and weight lifting outside of the team workouts to increase his performance, but Joe never got around to it. Fortunately, the two guys that could beat Joe graduated and he's on the varsity squad. He is pretty good and wins a lot of matches, and his coach thinks he might be able to place in the state tournament if he works hard, but he has still has not done anything extra on his own. He is beginning to wonder if he would like to wrestle in college.

Do you think that Joe is intrinsically motivated or are his motives more from extrinsic sources? Joe likes the attention that wrestling brings him and he likes to win. On the other hand, he was not as motivated when he wasn't winning and wouldn't make the necessary changes to increase his chances for success. He just waited for an opportunity to get on varsity.

Internal motivation is essential to success at the college level, because you have to thrive on what wrestling is made of. In college, it is less likely that you will have your parents at every match. Most of your competitions will be far away from your college or university, so your friends will not be there to watch you.

The concept of the team is quite different in college as well. In high school, you may have classes with a teammate or see each other in the halls. In college, depending on your area of study, you might not have any classes with teammates or even see each other except in practice. Some of your teammates might even be married, so the team probably will not hang out together like you might in high school.

It may take awhile to break into feeling like you are part of a team. College wrestlers don't exactly roll out the red carpet for an incoming freshman, because so many new guys quit that it is not worth their time to get to know them. In fact, the upperclassmen will take every opportunity in practice to see what you are made of, if you know what I mean. They don't want a teammate who isn't tough enough to take it.

Oh, and cheerleaders. You know the cute things that cheerleaders hang on your lockers before a match? Forget them! Most college wrestling teams don't even have cheerleaders. On the few teams that do have them, there isn't as much interaction between them and the wrestlers as there is in high school. Many of the college cheerleaders (of sports other than wrestling) seem to have boyfriends that *aren't* athletes; when they are at a competition they have a job to do, just like you.

How do you think Joe would like his experience as a college freshman? Are the things Joe likes about wrestling present in any abundance in the situation I have described? In my experiences as a college coach, I have seen many wrestlers who struggled in college, independent of how successful they had been in high school, because they were not intrinsically motivated. For every college all-American, there are probably 50 other guys with the talent to succeed at that level, but who lacked the internal drive.

You will probably find that the wrestlers at the highest levels are the ones who tend to have more intrinsic motivations than extrinsic motivations. This is because as you progress to the more elite levels, the external rewards are different and may be fewer than at other levels.

The point in saying all this is not to discourage you. You just have to know what you are getting into. If you have enjoyed the information in this book, then you are probably intrinsically motivated and it will work out well for you. College wrestling can be rewarding, but you have to know that you want to do it.

With this being the case, how do you know if college wrestling is for you? It starts with analyzing your own motives. It can be as simple as listing the things you like about wrestling in a piece of paper and deciding whether each is an intrinsic or an extrinsic motive and whether they will still be present at the college level.

Here is a very unscientific quiz that you can take. It is based on what I remember about my own motives, when I was making the transition from high school to college. I designed it to get you thinking about your own motives. For a more accurate assessment, develop several of your own questions and then sit down with your coach and talk about them.

Self assessment quiz (on a scale of 1-4)

    1=never   2=rarely   3=mostly   4=always

_____   I wrestle with a partner several days a week in the off-season whether or not a coach or other teammates are there.

_____   I condition and lift weights several days a week in the off-season without my coach telling me to.

_____   I like competing as much when family and friends are not in the crowd as I do when they are there.

_____   I like to go to wrestling practice even on my birthday or on a holiday.

_____   I think about what happens on the mat more than about how people will react to me after I win the match.

_____   Total score

17-20   Your motives make you a good candidate to be a college wrestler. You are more interested in wrestling for the sake of wrestling than the social aspects.

14-16   College wrestling might be for you, depending on the strength of the social influences at the college you select.

13 or less   College wrestling may not provide you with the same things you like about it now.

Wrestling in college is a great experience, but many of the rewards in college are different than those in high school. Most college wrestlers derive the value of their experience from internal feelings of accomplishment and pride in their hard work. This is not different from what many high school wrestlers value about their experience, but for many college wrestlers the internal rewards are a bigger part. There just isn't as much recognition and fan support for most college programs that are not big-time NCAA Division I programs.

On the other hand, college wrestling provides opportunities to meet some amazing people. Many of these individuals possess every-day greatness and commitment to excellence. There are relatively few college wrestlers compared to the number of college athletes in other sports. This means that future Olympians and world champions may be in the tournaments in which you compete. You may be one of them. It has been exciting for me to watch athletes I knew when I was in college move on in their careers and win medals in international competition.

WHERE CAN I WRESTLE IN COLLEGE?

Now that you've determined that your motivations for wanting to wrestle in college are in line with the internal nature of the rewards, you must determine if you have what it takes in the classroom and on the mat. If you have the right credentials, there will be a place for you.

Athletic programs that offer college wrestling fall into one of the following levels based on their respective national governing bodies. Most recognized is the National Collegiate Athletic Association (NCAA), which, for wrestling, supports three competition divisions based on the size and mission of the school. The National Association of Intercollegiate Athletics (NAIA) is the second governing body at the college level. Finally, the NJCAA, which is the National Junior College Athletic Association, governs junior college programs. Each category has specific attributes that allow wrestlers to select the program best for them.

Division I programs are usually the most competitive and large state universities comprise a lot of the membership. Athletes in this division are likely to be on some kind of athletic scholarship, and they are expected to produce, just like in any other job. If any collegiate wrestling receives a fan following, it is NCAA Division I. In fact, if you know anything about a college wrestling program that is more than 300 miles from your home, then it is probably a Division I program.

Division II is the second competition division offered by the NCAA. Many of the schools in this category are smaller, state-funded schools. Most of the students and a large majority of the athletes probably live within several hours' drive of the school. While some athletes are on sports scholarships at Division II schools, many are not. In most cases, Division II programs do not have the funding of Division I programs. At the collegiate level, the wrestling competitiveness between Division I and Division II is markedly different. While there are some Division II wrestlers that have won in tournaments featuring several, big-time Division I athletes, this is not common.

NCAA Division III is the third level of NCAA wrestling. In spite of the fact that the NCAA does not permit Division III programs to provide athletic scholarships, there is not as big a difference in competitiveness in wrestling between Divisions II and III that was seen between Divisions I and II. In fact, the best Division III wrestlers compete very well with the best Division II wrestlers.

NAIA wrestling teams have some of the same characteristics of NCAA II and NCAA III with respect to the size of the school and overall priority the school places upon its athletic program. Many of these programs offer wrestling scholarships. Junior college teams are two-year programs at schools designed to educate a local community. These are excellent places for some wrestlers to gain the necessary academic background for a four-year college. Many of the wrestlers in junior colleges are among the best in the country and eventually move on to big-time programs where they have tremendous success. Olympic champion Rulon Gardner and NCAA champion (and MMA title-holder) Brock Lesnar both started at the junior college level.

THE ODDS OF GETTING A SCHOLARSHIP

Does it seem like a lot of the wrestlers you know are getting a scholarship to wrestle somewhere? Of the several levels of college wrestling, only Division III does not have the option of providing some type of athletic scholarship. However, this is not a guarantee you will automatically receive a scholarship offer. Whether or not you can get a scholarship depends on a many factors.

First of all, many schools do not provide scholarships even though their respective governing bodies permit them to do so. Scholarship money is provided by each institution though the efforts of several organizations. Whether or not a college or university provides the scholarships reflects the mission of the school and where they prioritize their funding.

Secondly, the NCAA Division I has a limit of 9.9 scholarships for each wrestling team. (NAIA limits are different.) This means NCAA schools may provide scholarships up to the amount it would cost nine students to attend the school (in-state tuition, books, housing etc) and 9/10 of the money for one additional student. Unfortunately, it takes 10 athletes to fill a varsity roster. This means that technically, there isn't enough money for all of them to have a full scholarship, let alone members of the junior varsity or back-up wrestlers.

Many coaches break up their scholarships and give partial aid to wrestlers. A wrestler who attends a school that costs $20,000 a year can receive $300 a semester to cover the costs of books and be receiving a "scholarship." It might sound good to his friends back home, who may not know the dollar amount of the scholarship, but in terms of real financial assistance it is not significant. It is also common for coaches to recruit incoming freshmen on a commitment than they can eventually earn a scholarship.

Wrestling scholarships are not necessarily four-year commitments on the part of the institution. There may be situations where an incoming freshman receives an attractive package, and then has this scholarship reduced in subsequent years to provide money for new freshmen. In a way, this works the same for the college as having no scholarship as a freshman, and then giving one later. However, the family ends up scrambling to come up with the funds to attend school after a scholarship has been reduced.

When you hear someone received a wrestling scholarship, but you don't have the offers rolling, don't despair. As you can see there are different applications of a scholarship. Many of these reported in the local newspapers on not as impressive as they might at first appear.

BEING RECRUITED VS. WALKING ON

If a college coach contacts you and invites you to be on the team, whether or not there is scholarship money involved, you are, by definition, being recruited. When you join a team that has athletic scholarships, but you are not receiving one, it is considered "walking on."

What does it take to be recruited? Obviously, you have to be good. There are no brownie points for being a good guy, a hard worker or a well-rounded eagle scout. My experience is that most of the highly successful college wrestlers I met had a lot of other good things going for them. College coaches really don't care how good your mom and dad think you are.

Two critical attributes coaches want in a wrestler are the ability to win and having the academic discipline to stay eligible. In terms of winning, there are no "shouldas," "wouldas," or "couldas" considered. It doesn't matter if you were winning against a state champion in a match somewhere, and then lost in the final seconds. In fact, it doesn't really matter if you beat a state champion in a tournament somewhere, but didn't win state yourself. Most coaches will pass over you if you were picked to win the state, but didn't because you got sick. The bottom line is what you do, especially if you are a Division I prospect.

Unfortunately, winning a state championship is not a guarantee that you will be recruited by a college program. Colleges compete nationally, so the coaches compare you on a national level. This can be difficult. You might be a two- or three-time state champ from a state that does not have a reputation for producing elite college wrestlers, and not have a single college coach show interest in you. On the other hand you might be a state runner-up in a place like California, which is known for producing wrestlers that succeed at the college level, and have several coaches calling. This is why wrestling in the off-season in tournaments like the junior nationals, which is sponsored by USA Wrestling, can be valuable if you want to go to a Division I program.

College coaches are also interested in potential. I need to be careful when I say this because potential means different things to different people. What constitutes legitimate potential varies between coaches and programs. Big-time, Division I programs may see a one- or two-time state champion as an athlete who has the potential to become good enough to be a valuable training partner for best athletes in the program. On the other hand, smaller programs may see the same athlete as having the potential to make the varsity squad.

There is always the option to walk onto a program as long as the coach permits it and does not have a roster cap. You just have to determine if what you're undertaking will be worth your effort. If you are not the varsity guy, it means you are getting beat (and literally beat up) by the other wrestlers on a daily basis. This is a mentally challenging situation for a lot of wrestlers, because in college there are relatively few competition opportunities for non-varsity athletes. Typically, most of the open tournaments where non-varsity wrestlers can enter are in November and December. This makes it tough for the back-up wrestlers to stay motivated between January and March where there are lots of two-a-day practices and few opportunities for competition. This is probably the main reason why it is rare to see a non-varsity college wrestler stay in the program for four years, or even three years, for that matter.

Although the odds of being a successful college wrestler might seem bleak at first, you must remember that there is always room in any program for the best wrestlers. Doing the things I have described in this book will make you a better wrestler and help you develop the skills necessary to be successful in college. But you can't take this process lightly. I once read a sign in the wrestling room at the University of Wisconsin that sums up the approach you should take, "Never take on a vast project with a half-vast attitude."

CHAPTER 11
How to Be a
Blue-chip Recruit

Regardless of where you want to go to college, you should begin your preparation by immediately incorporating the things you have learned in this book. Beyond that, there are four things you can do to increase your chances of wrestling in college. First, you must prepare academically. Second, you should research college programs to identify the schools that offer programs that fit your needs. Third, evaluate the programs that interest you, and, fourth, market yourself to the coaches. These are each so important that I will discuss them individually in detail.

BE A STUDENT-ATHLETE NOT A DUMB JOCK!

When I was in high school, I was a just-get-by kind of student. Earning "C" grades would keep everyone off my back, and I could make these grades without studying. Unfortunately, it wasn't until I became a college coach that I realized how this lack of academic discipline was the limiting factor in my wrestling opportunities at the college level.

I wrestled at the NCAA Division II level, because I was not good enough as a wrestler to get a scholarship at the University of Wisconsin, the major Division I program in our state. Two other Division I programs offered me a partial scholarship, but I wasn't good enough academically to receive the financial aid that would have made it affordable. Some three- or four-time state champions may receive wrestling scholarships that cover all their expenses, but the small wrestling scholarships offered to me necessitated additional academic aid for which I was not qualified. Bottom line: I didn't get to go.

Although I had a great experience wrestling in two college programs that were suited to my ability, my horizons were somewhat limited coming out of high school. The only wrestling programs I knew about were the major Division I programs that received a lot of attention from the wrestling media. This is unfortunate, because there are many excellent programs that don't receive national attention for their wrestling. I became acquainted with one such team, the United States Air Force Academy, during my senior college season when I competed against their athletes and then later when I coached against them. What an institution!

One day it occurred to me that I had never lost a match to an academy wrestler, and I realized that I had been good enough to have made their varsity squad. In fact, when I was in college, I did beat a lot of guys from not-so-prestigious Division I programs, and I probably could have made any one of those teams. Unfortunately, during high school, I never considered any programs beyond my local area or the big-time programs that were always in the news.

The days of the "dumb jock" have come to an end for wrestling, because there are fewer opportunities to wrestle in college and the coaches can be more selective in their recruiting. When college coaches are interested in a prospect, they need to know the recruit will be able to stay eligible. Although simply maintaining eligibility represents a fairly minimal standard of achievement, it is necessary and many big-time coaches are reluctant to recruit students whose future eligibility might be in question. Some wrestlers feel than a "C" grade average is acceptable, because it is still "average." Earning a "C" grade in many high schools is possible with a minimal amount of effort, unless there is some kind of learning disability involved. In most cases, it does not reflect the work ethic or aptitude necessary to be successful in college where there are less people keeping track of your study habits.

Although average grades will keep you eligible to compete in high school, a good grade point average and national testing scores may be the ticket for you being able enroll at the college of your choice. Remember that I mentioned the limited amount of scholarships available at even the big-time programs? In all likelihood, you will not receive a "full-ride" scholarship to wrestle in college. Many college programs break up their wrestling scholarships, and in some cases academic scholarship and athletic scholarship can be combined. Academically based financial aid is especially important at the NCAA Division III level where there are no athletic scholarships.

Form a Partnership with Your Teachers

Getting good grades is a habit just like working hard in practice. Much of the battle to achieve good grades is won with effective time management. Think of how much you can accomplish physically when you run sprints for twenty minutes. The same can be said for studying. When I finally began studying, I was amazed at what I could accomplish in twenty- or thirty-minute blocks. There truly is a miracle in a minute.

Just a tiny little minute,

Only sixty seconds in it,

Forced upon me, can't refuse it,

Didn't seek it, didn't choose it,

But it's up to me to use it,

Give account if I abuse it.

Just a tiny little minute,

But eternity is in it.

Author unknown

Apply the same work ethic to studying for your classes that you do as you train for wrestling. You would not let a hard practice or a tough opponent get the best of you; do not let a hard class, a tough teacher or test get the best of you either.

Involving your teachers in your goal is an excellent strategy. My experience has been that most teachers entered the profession because they were passionate about helping students. Make an appointment to visit individually with the teachers of your toughest classes. Tell them about your goal to wrestle in college. Create a partnership where you are both working for the same goal. Teachers want students to succeed in their classrooms and in their personal lives. When you find out what it will take to earn an "A" in the class, commit to do everything necessary and then follow through. Do more than your part and the teacher will do his or hers.

I should mention that you must have demonstrated a habit of working hard to learn the material and an effort to make good grades before your visit with the teacher. If you are a "just-get-by" kind of student and you approach the teacher in the 11th hour of your junior or senior year, this will not work.

National Testing and the NCAA Clearinghouse

Standardized tests like the SAT and the ACT are used by most colleges and universities to help them select the applicants they will admit. In some cases, there are academic scholarships that are available based on having high enough scores.

These tests are usually available for you to take during your junior year in high school. However, there have been many situations when wrestlers I recruited did not take the test until their senior year. This was a challenging situation for wrestlers to whom I was intending to offer a scholarship during the NCAA's early signing period, which occurs in November of a prospect's senior year. Some universities will not accept a student without standardized test scores. When I was coaching I observed that wrestlers who were the most prepared for their college search had narrowed down their list to fewer than five schools and could provide those schools with a complete application, including national scores, sometime during August or September of their senior year.

If you take the SAT or ACT during your junior year and are not happy with your score, you can always retake it as a senior. In fact, there are even some national exams that you can take as a sophomore to prepare yourself further. Your school guidance counselor can give you further information about national testing.

Although it costs money to take these tests, it's an investment in yourself, like competing in summer tournaments, which make you a better wrestler. Early test attempts can reveal your deficiencies so you can prepare more in those subjects. There are even materials you can purchase to help you in your preparation.

Registering for the NCAA Clearinghouse at the beginning of your junior year in high school is another important act of preparation. The NCAA Clearinghouse is an online database that allows colleges and universities to verify that you meet the minimum high school academic requirements to be eligible to compete in college. There are five basic requirements you must meet to be eligible: 1) graduation from high school; 2) completion of specific core courses; 3) achieving a minimum grade point average; 4) receiving a minimum score on either the ACT or SAT test; and 5) documentation of your status as an amateur athlete. You can get more information and begin the registration process by visiting the NCAA Eligibility Center website at www.ncaaclearinghouse.net.

LEVELS OF COLLEGE WRESTLING PROGRAMS

Your final selection of a college will depend on where you get accepted, your ability to pay for it, and the program that matches your potential as an athlete. As I discussed in chapter ten there are several different classifications of college wrestling programs. Here are some of their attributes.

NCAA Division I

Every wrestler's goal should be to compete at the best NCAA Division I wrestling program available. I say the best Division I program, because there are big differences in the quality of programs. Some of these programs are not strong enough to beat Division II or NAIA teams. The big-time programs that get the media attention are national powerhouses on an annual basis. These are the programs to which I am referring.

There are several reasons why these programs provide the best wrestling experience for athletes. An important reason is the availability of off-season training opportunities. Usually the big-time programs have a club in place to help you in off-season competition and training, which is the time of year that you can make significant strides over opponents. Big-time programs are a hub for international-level athletes who are looking for a place to practice; interaction with them can only make you better. I felt a major limiting factor in my development in college was the lack of training and competition experiences I had in the off-season compared to what I had done in high school.

Generally, the big-time programs have more money, which is helpful in ways you might not even consider. One difference is in travel accommodations. Big-time programs are usually able to travel in a chartered bus or fly to competitions whereas smaller programs use vans to take trips upwards of one thousand miles or more. A small travel budget results in one of two situations. Small teams fundraise to take one or two flights in a season, and then spend the rest of the season wrestling locally where they see the same competition each week, or they make several thousand-mile trips in a van.

I remember one season when our Division II team made separate van trips from the Milwaukee, Wisconsin area to Sault St. Marie, Michigan; Edmond, Oklahoma; and the long one to Butte, Montana by way of Pueblo, Colorado. We left the tournament at about 11 p.m. after wrestling and drove from Montana to Milwaukee with no overnight stops. My coach did what he had to do to provide us with the competition necessary to help us and I will always appreciate that. Those experiences developed a tremendous camaraderie among the team and a sense of pride in what we were willing to go through for the chance to compete. I would unhesitatingly do it all again. Nevertheless, in most college programs those through-the-night drives are usually navigated by a coach or an athlete who has been awake all day (and up late the night before). There have also been accidents, including one that involved my former team the year after I transferred to another university.

Another reason a big-time program is an attractive choice is that the school is usually recognized by prospective employers. This isn't to say that schools in other classifications are not prestigious; outstanding schools are found in all divisions. However, the big-time wrestling programs are generally at schools where the quality of both the athletics and academics is very high.

NCAA Division II and III Programs

Programs associated with these divisions are great options for the right kind of athlete. In fact, they would be much better options for some of the wrestlers who compete at the Division I level. Unfortunately, many high school wrestlers and their parents will not consider a "D-II" or a "D-III" program; they want the prestige of Division I. I have often wondered about the quality of the wrestling experience of the Division I wrestlers who get beat by athletes from lower divisions.

Most athletes attend a school somewhat close to where they live. In my case I was fortunate that the area in which I grew up had several Division II and III programs. Had I ended up at a Division I program, I may not have been able to make the varsity, and I definitely would not have had the success on a national level. Knowing exactly where I ranked in comparison to the top wrestlers in my weight at the NCAA Division II level was tremendously motivating for me. This would not likely have happened if I had been in a small, Division I program, and not really sure how much further I had to progress to compete with the best wrestlers.

A great benefit of Division II and III programs is the overall size of the school, which can provide you with individual attention. In most cases, these schools are smaller than those associated with the big-time programs. This worked well for me. I mentioned previously that I was about a "C" student in high school. I lifted weights during my study halls, blew off preparing for the ACT, and rarely took a book home.

These negative habits persisted in college, where my first-semester grade point average was a lofty 1.57, which was helped tremendously by a five-credit "F" in chemistry and other not-so-impressive grades. This made me ineligible for wrestling, in spite of the fact that I had a wrestling scholarship. Some coaches might have cut their ties to me, especially at a big-time program, where the coach cannot spend all his time coddling a problem athlete. The individual attention of my coach and small student-to-teacher ratio in my school contributed to my getting back on track.

NAIA and Junior College Programs

At this point, I should mention I have grouped NAIA and junior college programs together, because they are governed by slightly different eligibility and recruiting rules than the NCAA. In terms of wrestling quality they are similar, and in many situations superior to some Division II and III programs.

There are some very good schools that are affiliated with the NAIA and their funding for scholarships is often better than some NCAA schools. Unfortunately, there are relatively few NAIA schools that sponsor wrestling. In fact, there have been situations where teams are allowed to enter more than one athlete at a weight class in the NAIA national tournament and where teammates have met in the finals.

A junior college may be an excellent option for you, if you don't have the necessary academic credentials to be accepted or eligible in a four-year program. This is one reason why there are so many tough wrestlers in the junior college ranks. These programs have been accurately described as feeder programs for Division I. A good junior college coach will not only recruit you, but he will also work hard to help you make the transition to a four-year college at the appropriate time.

Junior college may also be a good place to go for a year or two if you need the national-level exposure to college coaches that you might not have had out of high school. If you feel like you have the skills to wrestle at a higher level than that of the college that might be recruiting you, then go to a junior college and prove yourself there. Maybe your luck will improve. I should mention, however, that college coaches are good judges of talent. If you are only being recruited by one Division II, III or NAIA program, then be gracious enough to accept the offer. Legitimate Division I wrestlers are recruited by at least a few Division I programs and usually several lower-tier institutions.

College Clubs

Many universities host wrestling as a club sport, in which the wrestlers can compete against other colleges and universities in open events. In fact, the NCWA (National Collegiate Wrestling Association) has provided membership for several clubs and hosts a national championship. Teams within the NCWA are markedly different with regard to the organization of the program, the coaching staff, and the dedication of the athletes.

A few NCWA teams, including those that have won the national championship, are well organized and have an experienced coach. Most teams, however, are led by a student, who is usually a member of the team. Practices for the majority of club-level teams are typically two or three times per week, and these teams struggle to field enough wrestlers to fill the 10 weight classes in competitions. Although the student-coach and a few other team members may be dedicated, for many of the athletes, trips home on the weekend, going to a concert or other activities are higher priorities.

One way to gauge the quality of an NCWA program is to visit the team's website, many of which can be found at www.ncwa.net. More organized teams will have a roster, competition schedule, and results. Reviewing the schedule and the athletes' records will give you some idea of how often the wrestlers actually compete.

EVALUATING COLLEGE PROGRAMS

Evaluating which college program will be the best for you is not always easy. Why are perennial powerhouses like Iowa and Oklahoma

State able to win NCAA championships year after year? Those two programs have combined to win 69% of the national championships between 1928 and 2010. Oklahoma State won 34 team championships and Iowa won 23. In Appendix C, I have ranked the top 10 intercollegiate wrestling teams in their respective divisions based on their finishes in recent national tournaments. There have only been seven other teams to win championships. What keeps other universities from winning?

College programs differ markedly from each other due to the inequities in funding the respective athletic departments give to their wrestling programs. Ultimately, this support determines the quality of each student-athlete's experience. Successful programs, regardless of the division, have money and resources, which are the driving forces in college athletics. Without them, even good coaches struggle to win.

If colleges care about their program, the coaching staff will have pressure to win. Unfortunately, wrestling is not the highest priority in most college athletic departments. A few programs consistently win championships in their respective divisions. Other programs hope to produce some individual national champions and All-Americans on a somewhat regular basis. Unless you are fortunate enough to be recruited by one of the few wrestling powerhouses, it can be difficult to really know what you are getting into before you enroll in school. Team success with regard to wins and losses and the overall professional appearance of a program are good places to start.

Win-loss Record

When researching a team's competition success, there are three areas to consider. First of all, consider the team's dual-meet record. A strong dual-meet record in a tough conference (one where teams are consistently in the top 20 of Division I or the top 10 of Divisions II or III) suggests the team is balanced with good wrestlers and will have quality training partners for you. It also suggests that maintaining a varsity position is something that will require work, which will help you keep your edge.

The second area to consider is the number of national champions or All-Americans the team has produced in the last three to five years. Many teams do not have enough scholarship money to recruit good wrestlers at every weight, but such a team may consistently produce a few All-Americans or national champions. On the other hand, there may be some programs that consistently win duals in a weak conference, but rarely have an All-American. If I were an athlete and I had to choose between two programs, I would go to the team that produced the individual athletes.

Finally, you should consider trends for the program during three- or four-year cycles. There are some good coaches of teams at poorly supported programs. Due to the lack of scholarship money, many coaches can't get the top recruits each year, but they are good at developing hard-working wrestlers. Their win-loss record consistently improves until the third or fourth year when their "bumper crop" athletes are winning as a team and as individuals, and then the cycle begins again with a new group of incoming freshmen. The merits of such a program are not as obvious, because they don't get the media attention enjoyed by the powerhouse programs, but the quality of your wrestling experience on these teams can be excellent.

Big-time Feel of the Program

Although winning is the bottom line in college athletics, there is a certain amount of prestige that goes along with just being part of a team. The school's athletic mission and the way that the athletic department funds its programs create the big-time feel of the program. I mention big-time "feel," because you don't necessarily have to attend a large university to experience this. Many small schools run first-class wrestling teams. On the other hand, there are some large schools that don't care about wrestling and this is evident as well. You can learn a lot about how an athletic department prioritizes its wrestling program when you visit the wrestling website and research the structure of the coaching staff, the competition schedule and overall success.

When you first visit a wrestling team's website take note of whether it has the look of a sports website like the one you would see at a big-time university. It should have advertising associated with it—a sign that someone is willing to invest money into the program. The website should not look like something made from a software program a person would buy at an office supply store.

Another sure sign of a vibrant program is the relevancy of the stories on the site. You will notice that big-time Division I programs have new information about the team even in the summer months, whereas the sports information personnel of bush-league programs quit writing about the team as soon as the season ends. Programs with a big-time feel will have some stories about the athletes themselves, not just brief articles summarizing competitions.

The structure of the coaching staff reveals a lot about whether the school cares about its wrestling team. Such schools have a full-time head coach whose primary or sole responsibility is to coach. There may be successful teams with part-time coaches or full-time coaches with responsibilities in addition to wrestling, but the program's successes are generally more related to the talent of the team, not necessarily the fact that the school cares about its wrestling program. It's surprising how many Division II, III and NAIA wrestling programs are run by part-time coaches or someone who balances his time between several duties.

You can also learn a lot about a wrestling program by looking at its competition schedule. True big-time programs at the Division I level will have events that allow them to compete against teams from the entire country several times throughout the season. Programs at the Division

II, III or NAIA levels have smaller travel budgets and compete regionally. This means they see the same people several times a season. When I was coaching, it was not uncommon to have athletes from our conference who had wrestled the same opponent five or six times in a season. However, smaller programs with a big-time feel generally fundraise or do whatever it takes to get at least a few trips a year to different parts of the country to expose their wrestlers to new competition. Be careful, however, some of the small programs will put a token "trip" on the schedule each season to make the athletes and recruits think they are getting the big-time experience.

Selecting a college is one of the most important decisions of your life. Several factors will be important. I have focused on the merits of the wrestling program. Obviously, academics play a huge role. Some people will tell you that the academics are the most important factor. Generally, this comes from the "either or" mentality of brainiacs, with limited sports experience, or by coaches who hide behind the academic merits of their school, because their sports programs are weak.

High-level wrestling can coexist with an outstanding educational experience. Division I national champions have come from outstanding academic institutions and many NCAA champions and All-Americans (from state schools) have gone on to prestigious professions in medicine, law, research, and business. What you make of your college experience is up to you. Just look for programs that have produced alumni with the kind of academic and athletic credentials that you would like to achieve and apply to those schools.

CHAPTER 12
Marketing Yourself and Visits
Wined, Dined & Signed

Your success will be in direct proportion to your willingness to take chances.
-Dr. Harold Cheuvront, Dean of Students Colorado School of Mines

CONTACTING A COLLEGE COACH

Have you ever wondered why one wrestler might have college coaches calling with scholarship offers and another, equally talented, wrestler seems to get no interest? While most college coaches will take notice of a three-time state champion, a wrestler from a tough wrestling state who has placed in the top three or four at the state tournament a few times and possibly at the junior national tournament can develop into a great college wrestler. Bruce Baumgartner, a former Team USA heavyweight who won four Olympic medals, never won a high school state championship. There are other college champions with similar stories. The difference comes down to marketing and what the customer, in this case the college coach, needs in his program. Most wrestlers do very little to market themselves to college coaches, but you can do several things that will help you get noticed by prospective coaches. (Use the worksheet in Appendix C to keep yourself on track to complete all the necessary steps to be a recruitable wrestler.)

If you are good enough—a top prospect for big-time programs—the coaches will contact you. You will know if you fall into this category, because coaches will initiate phone contacts with you before the beginning of your senior year. NCAA rules will allow coaches to contact you by telephone or in person after June 15 of your junior year in high school. (NAIA rules are different, so if you hear from an NAIA coach but not an

NCAA coach that might be why.) Prospective college athletes can sign a National Letter of Intent as early as November of their senior year in high school, so most coaches are very busy making phone calls and visits to athletes' homes in August and September. Wrestlers who are not heavily recruited during the early signing period in November will sometimes be recruited later and may have an offer extended during the April signing period.

You shouldn't wait until your senior year, however, to find out if you will be a top recruit. There are a few reasons for this. First of all, it is not only the college sports teams that are looking to recruit good athletes to their school, college admissions offices are hoping to attract the best students as well. If you apply to schools early and qualify for academic scholarships, you have a better chance of receiving aid. Secondly, if you are not a multi-time state champion or have not won or placed high in the junior national tournament, then there is a good chance that you will not be recruited by top programs and that you will have to market yourself to get the attention of college coaches. You need to be on their radar during your junior and senior year.

To get recruited you must be the kind of wrestler in high school that a college coach would want. College wrestlers are dedicated; they train hard and they were winners in high school. You have to make the commitment to wrestle in as many summer tournaments as you can and attend as many camps as you can. Don't waste a college coach's time unless you are willing to make this kind of commitment and you have had at least some success in your high school state tournament or a national tournament.

Secondly, you can initiate the contact with the college coaching staff. While NCAA rules prohibit the coach from calling you at various times, you can contact them any time. You need to be smart about this, however. The last thing a busy college coach needs is to have a high school wrestler calling him after every match. This is why it is probably best to initiate a contact by a letter sometime in the beginning of your junior year. I would only do this if you have placed in the state in your freshman or sophomore years. What would you write in the letter if you had not placed in the state? "I like long walks on the beach..."

Most coaches hate paperwork and your letter will be quickly passed to an assistant, if the coach has one. The main reason you are making this contact is so that a member of the coaching staff will recognize your name when he hears it at the state tournament. Send a cover letter and your one-page wrestling resume with the following information:

- Your name, address and telephone number
- Year in school and expected graduation date
- Your coach's name and phone number
- Weight class and accomplishments such as state or national placing or wins over ranked opponents
- GPA and courses taken, specifically English, math and science
- Scores on ACT or SAT, if you have taken them

Here is an example of a cover letter to send.

Dear Coach Jones,

I am writing to introduce myself and to let you know of my interest in your wrestling program. Currently I am beginning my junior year at Sparta High School in Sparta, Wisconsin. This season I will compete at 171 pounds and I am looking to improve upon my 4th place finish last season in the state tournament at 160 pounds. My overall high school record is 62-11 and I compete in freestyle and Greco tournaments in the spring. Last summer I made the junior national team.

I am including my biographical and academic information for your review. My parents and I are planning to visit your campus on November 5, and I would welcome an opportunity to visit you or a member of your staff in person.

Best of luck to you in your recruiting and competition this season.

Sincerely,

Caleb Smith

171-pound wrestler

Sparta High School

Do everything you can to make a visit to the schools you are interested in during your junior year. It will help you narrow your options during your senior year and meeting a coach in person will make it more likely that he will remember you at the state tournament.

It would also be a good idea to send a follow-up letter (and resume in case the first was lost) about two weeks before the state tournament inviting the coach to watch for you. Again, this letter should be short like the following example:

Dear Coach Jones,

I am writing as a follow-up to the letter I sent last fall and to invite you to watch me in the upcoming state tournament. My record is 28–1 and I am looking forward to improving upon last year's 4th place finish. I still compete at 171 pounds and our school competes in the 4A class, which starts on February 22 at 10:00 a.m.

Included are an update of my GPA, the scores I received on my ACT and the courses I have been taking that are required by the NCAA Clearinghouse.

Best of luck to you and your wrestlers in the upcoming conference tournament.

Sincerely,

Ryan Eckell

Oak Creek High School Wrestler

608-420-3211

Ideally, the college coach will send you a recruiting questionnaire and some information about the school after he receives your letter. The NCAA is very specific about the kind of material the coach can send you at various times, so if some of the things you receive are kind of generic, don't be offended. If the coach contacts you by phone before wrestling season starts your senior year, then that's a good sign. There is a good chance, however, that the coach may not contact you. If this is the case, send follow-up letters during your senior year that update the information sent in during your junior year.

PREPARING FOR A PRODUCTIVE CAMPUS VISIT

Nothing can tell you more about a college than what you can learn by visiting the campus. If you are being recruited, then coaches will invite you to visit and sometimes pay all or a part of NCAA-approved expenses. When the coach pays expenses, the visit is referred to as an "official visit," and you are limited to this one time each at five different schools. This is why it is important to narrow down your list of potential schools before you are offered an expense-paid visit. You can visit a school at your own expense as frequently as you would like, however. If you live a reasonable distance from the colleges you are considering or you can afford to travel there, it will be worth your time to make the trip.

A productive campus visit can not only inform you about the merits of the school, it can also fully sell the coaching staff on how well you will fit into their program. In many ways, a campus visit is like when a company brings candidates in for a job interview. You should prepare in similar ways. Before the visit, you should review the wrestling team's webpage on the college's website to learn about the team and the staff. This will help you feel more comfortable when you meet them.

After visiting the team's webpage, make sure to review other web pages for the school including those for the admissions office and the one that is usually called "academics." The admissions office's page will have the important dates for application deadlines, while the academics page will list the degree programs. Make notes of anything you have questions about, so you can ask the appropriate person during your visit.

Unless you are in a position to make several campus visits at your own expense, you get only one shot, so make sure to contact all the important individuals during your visit. Each wrestling program will do things a little differently, but all visits arranged by the school should have similar appointments on your schedule. When I hosted students during visits, I made sure to include the following activities on an itinerary I sent to the athletes before they arrived:

- Visit with an admissions officer who could discuss admission policies and deadlines
- Attendance at a class with one of our wrestling team members
- Observation of a training activity or competition (NCAA rules won't allow recruits to actually participate in a workout.)
- An introduction to a member of the athletic administration (preferably the compliance officer), who could tell them about eligibility requirements and some school-specific policies or programs
- An overnight with a current team member and meals in our dining facilities
- A social event that would include members of other teams or other students

If a school-arranged visit is missing an appointment with someone you feel you need to see, politely ask if you can make some time during the visit to meet that individual. Whoever is arranging the visit can usually add it to your schedule.

When you initiate your own visit, you can include as many things as you feel are necessary. You probably will not be able to stay overnight on campus and you may not be able to watch a team activity. However, most university officials will meet with you for 15 minutes, if you give them a few weeks' notice. Whether you attend an official visit or one on your own, be sure to send a "thank you" note afterwards identifying a few things you liked about the school and wrestling program.

What Not to do on Your Campus Visit

Obviously you want your visit to be as enjoyable and productive as possible. Generally, everything goes well. Occasionally, however, situations arise that create misunderstandings or incidents regretted by the recruit, the wrestling program or both. Here are a few things to avoid during your visit.

First of all, don't bring up the subject of scholarships to a coach or ask a member of the team how much he is getting. Wrestling programs that have scholarship money do not bring recruits to campus unless they plan to provide some kind of aid. Let the coach determine the appropriate time to discuss this. His time frame will probably be similar to that of other coaches who may be offering you a scholarship. If you don't get an offer from him on that timeline, then he may not be offering one. If you have scholarship offers from other schools, but you have not heard from a coach who has recruited you, then it would be a good time to follow-up with coach.

Secondly, don't be cool or aloof during your campus visit. It is natural to be a little nervous about making the visit, because you want the coach to like you and the team members to accept you. Some wrestlers try to hide this by showing very little emotion or interest during the visit. That might be a good defense mechanism, but it is hard for coaches to read that. I could never tell if the athlete was just quiet or didn't like what we had to offer. This doesn't mean you have to be overly chatty either. You're not a cheerleader; just find a balance between responding to every question with a one-syllable answer and talking too much. The most important thing is to be yourself. You want to find out before you enroll in school if the program is a fit for you.

Finally, don't get into any trouble while you are on your visit. Don't even think about touching alcohol and avoid any extracurricular dating activities. Remember, your visit is a professional activity. The kind of drinking that happens on a college campus would not happen during the interview process for a legitimate professional organization. In most cases, you will not be legally old enough to drink, anyway. The few cases where prospects get into trouble are unfortunate, because, in most cases, the situation is an isolated mistake and not reflective of the athlete's character. Don't let your reputation become tarnished because you felt pressured to do something to fit in.

Drinking and College Wrestling

I am always thrilled when I meet a high school wrestler who is disciplined in his or her diet, exercise routine and who tells me that he or she has never tried alcohol. Perhaps you are one of these athletes. Unfortunately, there are stories where a straight-laced athlete gets to college and begins using alcohol and other drugs. I use the term "other drugs" to be clear that alcohol is a drug in the same way that marijuana is a drug. The difference is that alcohol consumption is accepted by society. However, your goals make you different from the average person and alcohol will not help you realize your dreams.

When you get to college, you might see athletes who use drugs and who may appear to be successful. Because of their successes, you might be tempted to begin using yourself. Before you take your first drink, however, ask yourself what you will gain from doing it. Is there any benefit to lowering standards you have set for yourself? People notice when someone holds themselves to a higher standard and they will respect you for it. You have the rest of your life to drink, if that is important to you, but once you've taken a nip, you can never again say, "I've never touched alcohol, and alcohol has never touched me."

EAT YOUR ELEPHANT ONE BITE AT A TIME

At this point, the world of college wrestling might sound complicated. It is a world of adults where your wrestling meets professionalism. Wrestling at the college level becomes your job and much will be expected of you. With relatively few college wrestling programs out there, opportunities are rare. Nevertheless, somebody gets to do it, and it might as well be you.

If you are like I was when I graduated from high school, then you are probably wondering if you have what it takes to succeed at the next level. When I began college wrestling (and high school, for that matter), I noticed how good everyone else seemed to be. We had a great wrestler on my college team, who was about a year ahead of me in the program. He was so good that in spite of only wrestling for the last half of the season, he placed in the nationals. Unfortunately, after he finished that season, he

didn't come back. I thought it was strange until I saw a similar situation a few years later on another team.

In my first NCAA Division II championship match I ran into a buzz saw from Central Missouri State. This guy beat me badly and completely out-worked me. Given the fact that I prided myself on my conditioning, this came as a bit of a shock and was more than a little depressing. I'd never even heard of the guy. Worst of all, he still had two more years of eligibility! Imagine my surprise when I learned the following season that he quit the team.

These two examples illustrate the fact that many of the talented wrestlers you meet in the beginning of wrestling season don't stick with the program until they graduate. I have noticed that many state and national champions are good wrestlers who outlasted more talented competitors who were waylaid by girlfriends or parties or who simply left wrestling for other pursuits. If you are willing to stick with it, you will generally achieve more than you thought was possible. Eat your elephant one bite at a time.

My experiences as a coach have led me to believe that most wrestlers with college potential are better than they think. They are better at adapting to the demands of college than they expected, and they meet the challenges successfully. Keys for your success will be for you to make a long-term commitment to finishing the program and then being true to yourself. Success in college wrestling boils down to picking the school that is appropriate for you, and then working your butt off in the classroom and on the mat when you get there. If you are willing to do the things recommended in this book, and if you are willing to take some risks, then you will do fine. It will be an awesome experience. Pack your bags and take me with you!

Super Circuits That Rock

INSTRUCTIONS:

- Intensities for the cardio intervals for each of these circuits are based on how hard you feel like you are working on a scale of 1-10. Level 1 is the effort of doing nothing and 10 is the hardest sprint you could maintain for about 45 seconds.

- Rotate from exercise to exercise without a rest.

- Circuit time does not include a warm-up or cool down

BEGINNER-LEVEL CIRCUITS

Machine-based Super Circuit

Time: About 20 minutes

Equipment:
- Jump rope* or elliptical trainer, Air Dyne, rowing machine, etc.
- About 12 weight machines

Sets: 1 per exercise

Reps: 10-12 at 60% of maximum

Cardio interval: 45 seconds at level 6

Cardio mode: Schwinn Air Dyne, elliptical trainer, stationary bike, jump rope*

NOTE: Alternate upper- and lower-body exercises

*Progress gradually with jump rope to avoid an impact-related overuse injury; work towards high-knee jumping with an alternating leg (running in place) pattern.

Tempo-based Super Circuit

Time: About 25 minutes

Equipment:
- Cardio equipment or a jump rope
- Weight room free weights

Sets: 2 per exercise

Reps: 12-15

Rep tempo: Raise weight 1 second, Lower weight 2 seconds

Cardio interval: 45 seconds at level 7

Exercises: Squat, Bench Press, Lunge, Bent-over Row, Leg Flexion, Low Bridge Shoulder Touches

NOTE: Alternate upper- and lower-body exercises

INTERMEDIATE-LEVEL CIRCUITS

Muscle-group Super Circuit

Time: About 25 minutes

Equipment:
- Jump rope or other cardio equipment
- Pull-up bar, dipping bar, dumbbells of various weights, stability ball

Sets: 1 per exercise

Reps: 12 at 80% of maximum

Cardio interval: 60 seconds at level 8

Exercise combos:
- Bent-arm jackknives, Prone snow angels, Dynamic trunk rotations
- Deadlift, Lunge (6 per leg), Stability ball single-leg curl (six per leg)
- Reverse pull-up knee lifts, Alternating dumbbell upright row, Stability ball reverse fly
- Dips, Stability ball incline press, Single-arm dumbbell fly (six per arm)

NOTE: Perform a "giant set" of 3 exercises in a row between each aerobic interval.

Core-strength Super Circuit

Time: About 25 minutes

Equipment:
- One stability ball
- One medicine ball or a dumbbell at a weight you can do a single-arm curl for 3 sets of 10

Sets: 1 per exercise

Reps: 16 (8 each direction)

Cardio interval: two minutes at level 8

Exercises:
- Dynamic trunk rotations
- Supine DB swings
- Prone rocking
- Prone pike
- Prone J-strokes
- Back extension
- Reverse wood choppers

ADVANCED-LEVEL CIRCUITS

Balance-based Super Circuit

Time: About 20 minutes

Equipment:
- Cardio equipment or jump rope
- One stability ball
- One dumbbell that you can do a single-arm curl for 3 sets of 10

Sets: 1 per exercise

Reps: 8 total (or 8 with each limb for single-limb exercises)

Cardio interval: 90 seconds at level 8

Exercises:

- Ball balance overhead squats
- Ball bridge double-knee curl
- Ball-balance single-arm lateral and front raises
- Ball-balance single-arm curl-press
- Shock lockouts alternately landing with one hand or fist in the ball
- Ball-balance single-arm bench press or fly
- Handstand balance (work up to 15 seconds)

Ninja Super Circuit

Time: About 30 minutes

Equipment:

- Cardio equipment or jump rope
- Two stability balls
- Towel
- Pull-up Bar

Sets: 1 per exercise

Reps: 8 total (or 8 with each limb for single-limb exercises)

Cardio interval: 90 seconds at level 8

Exercises:

- Step up on ball without using hands
- Ball balance squats w/ alternating dumbbell front and lateral raises
- Ball bridge single-knee curl
- Ball balance (standing on ball) reverse flies
- Two-ball push-ups (fist in ball)
- Two-ball cross rollouts
- Single-leg prone pike
- Ball rollout plank
- Towel saws

Annual Strength & Conditioning Program

This program is based on a training cycle with critical competitions in late February or early March. Sample workouts are only examples of exercises you could do. Frequently vary the exercises, but generally stick to the set and rep schemes for each type of lift.

OFF-SEASON PHASE I

April 1 - May 30

Goals: Increase strength, avoid increasing unnecessary body fat

Days per week: 3

Total Body and Core Lifts: 3-5 sets of 6-8 reps of deadlift, back squat, bench press, bent-over row

Auxiliary Lifts and Rotational Exercises: 2 x 10 of any single-joint or stability–limited exercises

Conditioning: Any mode you choose 20 minutes

Sample Workouts

April 1-15	May 1-15
Warm-up 10 minutes easy cycling	Warm-up 10 minutes easy jogging
Deadlift 3 x 6	Deadlift 4 x 6
Back Squat 3 x 8	Back Squat 4 x 6
Bench Press 3 x 8	Bench Press 4 x 6
Bent-over Row 3 x 8	Bent-over Row 4 x 6
Reverse wood choppers 2 x 12	Supine dumbbell rotation 2 x 10
Arm flexion/extension 2 x 12	Bent-arm pull-up hold 1 x 60 seconds
Leg Curl 2 x 10	Cool down 10 minutes easy jogging.

ACTIVE REST I

June 1-15

Goals: Keep active with other sports, stay out of the weight room

OFF-SEASON PHASE II

June 16 - August 15

Goals: Increase power, increase conditioning intensity

Days per week: 3 (two lifting and one conditioning)

Power Lifts: 3-4 sets of 3-6 reps of power clean from knees

Power Exercises and Plyometrics: 3-5 sets x 10 contacts of penetration jumps, lateral bounding, clapping push-ups, etc.

Total Body and Core Lifts: 3-5 sets of 6-8 reps overhead squat, front squat, incline bench press, dumbbell row

Auxiliary Lifts and Rotational Exercises: 1-2 x 10 of any single-joint or stability–limited exercises

Conditioning: 3 sets 6 minutes of hard conditioning with three-minute rest once per week

Sample Workouts

Lifting Day (June 16, 18*)	Conditioning Day
Warm-up: 5 minutes of cardio	Warm-up 5 minutes easy cardio
Power clean 3 x 6 @75% 1-RM	Dynamic stretches
Overhead squat 3 x 5 @ estimated 10-RM weight	6 minutes of hard cardio (100% effort)
Incline Press 3 x 8-RM	3 minutes walking recovery
Dumbbell Row 3 x 8 (load you can use with good form)	Repeat two more times
Prone Pike 2 x 10	Cool down with light walking
*Use 80% of June 16 loads	

ACTIVE REST II

August 16-30

Goals: Keep active with other sports, stay out of the weight room

PRE-SEASON PHASE I

September 1 - November 1

Goals: Increase power and Strength; Increase lactic acid tolerance, Prepare body for increased training demands of wrestling practices
Days per week: 4 (two lifting and two conditioning)
Power Lifts: 3-4 sets of 3-6 reps of power clean, from the knees
Power Exercises and Plyometrics: 3-5 sets x 10 contacts of penetration jumps, lateral bounding, clapping push-ups, etc.
Total Body and Core Lifts: 3-5 sets of 6-8 reps deadlift, overhead squat, front squat, back squat, incline press, dumbbell row, and upright row
Auxiliary Lifts and Rotational Exercises: 3 x 10 of any single-joint or stability–limited exercises
Conditioning: Interval sprints on track or trail

Sample Workouts

Strength Day (Monday and Thursday)	Conditioning Days (Tuesday and Friday)	
	Week 1 (Sept 1-7)	*Week 2 (Sept 9-16)*
Warm-up 5 minutes	4 x 6s w/ 18s rest	4 x 6s w/ 18s rest
Hang Clean from knee 3 x 5	2 x 20s w/60s rest	3 x 20s w/60s rest
of estimated 8-RM	1 x 40s w/80s rest	2 x 40s w/80s rest
Clapping Push-ups with feet		
on block 3 x 10		
Front Squat 3 x 5-RM		
One-arm incline press 3 x 6-RM	*Week 3 (Sept 17-23)*	*Week 4 (Sept 24-30)*
Dumbbell Upright Row 3 x 8-RM	4 x 6s w/ 18s rest	4 x 6s w/ 18s rest
Prone J-strokes 3 x 10	4 x 20s w/60s rest	4 x 20s w/60s rest
Cool down	3 x 40s w/80s rest	4 x 40s w/80s rest

WRESTLING INITIATION PHASE
November 1-15

Goal: Avoid overtraining during first weeks of practice, no extra strength or conditioning workouts.

COMPETITION PHASE
November 15-January 15

Goals: Increase strength and power

Days per Week: 2

Power Lifts: 3-5 sets of 3-5 reps of Power Clean or Hang Clean

Power Exercises and Plyometrics: 2-3 sets x 10 contacts of penetration jumps, lateral bounding, clapping push-ups etc, medicine ball/sandbag tosses

Total Body and Core Lifts: 3-5 sets of 4-6 reps deadlift, overhead squat, front squat, back squat, incline press, dumbbell Row, upright row

Auxiliary Lifts and Rotational Exercises: 2 x 15-20 of any single-joint or stability –limited exercises

Conditioning: Sprints after practice unless more conditioning is needed

Sample Workouts

December 1	January 15
Warm-up 5 min on bike	Warm-up 5 min on bike
Hang clean front squat 5 x 5 @ estimated 8-RM	Sandbag granny toss* 3 x 5 as high as possible
Twisting Lunge w/weight plate 3 x 8	Ball single-leg lateral wall slide 2 x 15
Towel pull-ups 2 sets of max reps (goal of 15)	Bent-over Row 5 x 6
Bench press 5 x 5	Shock-lockouts on stability ball 1 x 10
Ball bridge single-knee curl 2 x 15	Elbow flexion/extension 2 x 15
Cool Down	Cool down

*Using a 20- to 40-pound sandbag, start with it on the floor between your feet. In one motion throw it as high as possible being careful not to let it land on you.

PEAKING PHASE

Goals: Increase power-endurance/strength-endurance and maximize lactic acid tolerance

Days per Week: 2 (72 hours minimum between strength and conditioning sessions)

Power Lifts: Timed exercises on hang clean

Power Exercises and Plyometrics: 2-3 sets x 10 contacts of any plyometrics exercises with 30-60 seconds between sets

Total Body, Core, Auxiliary, Stability-limited Exercises: Performed for about one-minute each with 30-60 seconds rest or in a timed circuit.

Conditioning: Peaking Interval Training

Sample Workouts

Power-/Strength-Endurance

Warm-up 5 minutes choice of exercise

Hang Clean 3 x 45 seconds (10-12 reps) @50-60% estimated 1-RM with one minute rest between sets

Penetration jumps with weighted vest or light dumbbells 3 x 14-16 reps with one minute rest

Squat-thrust Pull-ups 3 x 12-15 with body weight with 45-second rest

Stability ball prone pike 3 x 15 with body weight with 45-second rest

Cool down

Peaking Interval Training

Warm-up 5 minutes choice of exercise

Seven 1-minute full-effort sprints on Air Dyne or elliptical trainer with 3-min recovery between sprints

Cool Down

APPENDIX C
Top Ten Intercollegiate
Wrestling Programs by Division

Note: Rankings are based on finishes in national tournaments held from 2006-2010.

NCAA Division I

School	National Championships	Finishes in Top 3	Conference
Iowa	3	3	Big Ten
Iowa State	0	3	Big 12
Oklahoma State	1	1	Big 12
Minnesota	1	2	Big Ten
Cornell	0	1	The Ivy League
Ohio St	0	2	Big Ten
Oklahoma	0	1	Big 12
Nebraska	0	0	Big 12
Missouri	0	1	Big 12
Michigan	0	0	Big Ten

NCAA Division II

School	National Championships	Finishes in Top 3	Conference*
Nebraska-Omaha	3	5	MIAA
Nebraska-Kearney	1	4	Rocky Mountain
Minnesota State University-Mankato	0	2	Northern Sun
University of Central Oklahoma	1	1	Lone Star
Adams State College	0	0	Rocky Mountain
University of Pittsburg Johnstown	0	0	WVIAC
Augustana College	0	0	Northern Sun
Newberry College	0	0	South Atlantic
Upper Iowa University	0	0	Northern Sun
Western State College	0	0	Rocky Mountain

Appendix C: Top Ten Intercollegiate Wrestling Programs by Division

NCAA Division III			
School	National Championships	Finishes in Top 3	Conference
Wartburg College	3	5	Iowa Intercollegiate
Augsburg College	2	5	Minnesota Intercollegiate
University of Wisconsin-La Crosse	0	5	Wisconsin Intercollegiate
Delaware Valley College	0	0	Middle Atlantic
Coe college	0	0	Iowa Intercollegiate
Luther College	0	0	Iowa Intercollegiate
Ithaca College	0	0	Empire 8
SUNY Cortland	0	0	SUNYAC
Elmhurst College	0	0	CCIW
Cornell College	0	0	Iowa Intercollegiate

*In NCAA divisions II and III not all conferences sponsor wrestling. In Division II, qualification berths to the national tournament are contested in one of four regional tournaments. Four wrestlers in each weight class from each regional advance to the national tournament. Qualification in Division III is similar to Division I. In many cases conference tournaments serve as qualifiers in conferences that host wrestling. In other situations a qualifying tournament is held with teams from several schools. The number of qualifiers from each conference or qualifying tournament is based on the performances of wrestlers from the conference in previous national tournaments.

Appendix C: Top Ten Intercollegiate Wrestling Programs by Division

NAIA			
School	National Championships	Finishes in top 3	Conference
Lindenwood University	3	4	Heart of America
Dickinson State	0	2	Dakota Athletic
McKendree University	0	2	American Midwest
Missouri Valley College	0	0	Heart of America
Dana College	1	1	Great Plains Athletic
Southern Oregon University	0	2	Cascade Collegiate
University of Great Falls	0	1	Frontier
Embry Riddle Aeronautical Univ. (AZ)	0	1	N/A
Notre Dame College (OH)	1	1	American Mideast
University of the Cumberlands (KY)	0	1	Mid-south

Junior College (NJCAA)		
School	National Championships	Finishes in top 3
Iowa Central Community College	4	5
Labette Community College	0	3
North Idaho College	0	3
Harper College	1	2
Nassau Community College	0	1
Colby Community College	0	0
Clackamas Community College	0	0
Ellsworth Community College	0	0
North Iowa Community College	0	0
St. Louis Community College-Merramac	0	1

Worksheet and Timeline for College Enrollment Planning

Freshman Year	Date Completed/Notes
Visit www.eligibilitycenter.org to learn NCAA eligibility requirements.	
Summer after freshman year wrestle in the Junior Nationals if possible.	
Sophomore Year	
Beginning of year visit high school guidance counselor to talk about courses you need to take for NCAA eligibility.	
Wrestle in the Junior Nationals if possible.	
Junior Year	
Beginning of year review courses with guidance counselor.	
Beginning of the year register for the NCAA Clearinghouse at www.eligibilitycenter.org	
Register for the ACT and SAT tests and take them.	
List your top 10 choices for places to attend college and wrestle.	
Review colleges' admissions office websites and complete the prospective-student questionnaires.	
Send each coach a letter of introduction. (See Ch. 12)	

Before state tourney invite college coaches to watch you. (See Ch. 12)	
Reduce college choices to five and plan to visit as many as possible.	
Attend a wrestling camp at the school you are most interested in.	
Summer: Apply to your top two college choices.	
Wrestle in the Junior Nationals if possible.	
Senior Year	
Review courses with guidance counselor in beginning of year.	
Register to retake the ACT or SAT, if necessary.	
Send letters to any college coaches who may not have contacted you.	
Jan-April: Complete financial aid applications at www.fafsa.gov.	

INDEX

ABOUT THE AUTHOR

Steve Kimpel teaches in the Exercise and Sports Science department at Brigham Young University-Idaho. As an athlete he was a three-time collegiate All-American and trained briefly with Greco-Roman athletes at the Olympic Training Center in Colorado Springs, Colorado. Prior to his current position, he was the head wrestling coach at Wabash College and at Colorado School of Mines. In 2007 he received the Coaching Excellence Award from the National Wrestling Coaches Association.

He holds a PhD in education with an emphasis in exercise physiology from the University of Idaho and is a Certified Strength and Conditioning Specialist for the National Strength and Conditioning Association. His training articles have appeared on intermatwrestle.com and in Wrestling USA magazine. He has lectured internationally on the topics covered in this book and he has been a technique clinician for high school wrestling coaches' association conferences in Colorado, Indiana and Wisconsin.

Steve and his family reside in Rexburg, Idaho.

CPSIA information can be obtained at www.ICGtesting.com
Printed in the USA
LVOW061526230113

316964LV00004B/587/P